The Digital Revolution and the Coming of the Postmodern University

In recent years, the powerful social, cultural and economic changes wrought by digital technology have led many to forecast the end of the university as we know it. This book, for the first time, employs extensive research and case studies to explain why these predictions, even if perhaps somewhat premature, are on solid ground.

The Digital Revolution and the Coming of the Postmodern University shows how the internet, high-speed electronic communications, and personal computers necessitate a radical rethinking of what is meant by 'higher education'. The book calls into question both the traditionalist's scepticism about the benefits of new technology and the corporate e-learning advocate's failure to grasp that education is more than what happens on a computer screen. The author provides concrete data and models for more democratic, restructured systems of instruction that not only take advantage of advanced learning technologies, but promote the globalization of higher education.

This book is an essential read for anyone concerned about the future of higher education.

Carl A. Raschke is Professor of Religious Studies at the University of Denver. He is an internationally known and often quoted analyst of contemporary affairs and culture, who has published widely on subjects ranging from postmodernism to the reform of higher education.

[handwritten annotations:]
educational (teacher/student to country)
temporal (asynchronicity)
spatial (to a user extent)
unreadable thread fragments of thought

lack of unity both strength + weakness?
week 1 summary - diversity of perspective +
significant depth of experience by main
resource of the course. A de-centred Protean
'postmodern' disposal (p.5) as many (multi-
knowledge + education in the digital age?   centred)
A 'knowledge space' (Levy) v. classroom room
the

The Digital Revolution and the Coming of the Postmodern University

Carl A. Raschke

[handwritten notes:]
Digital pedagogy ideas
the 'transactional archetype' p56
weblog
Discourse
not VLES

RoutledgeFalmer
Taylor & Francis Group

LONDON AND NEW YORK

First published 2003 by RoutledgeFalmer
11 New Fetter Lane, London EC4P 4EE

Simultaneously published in the USA and Canada
by RoutledgeFalmer
29 West 35th Street, New York, NY 10001

Reprinted 2003

RoutledgeFalmer is an imprint of the Taylor & Francis Group

© 2003 Carl A. Raschke

Typeset in Sabon and Gill by BC Typesetting, Bristol
Printed and bound in Great Britain by
TJ International Ltd, Padstow, Cornwall

British Library Cataloguing in Publication Data
A catalogue record for this book is available from the British Library

Library of Congress Cataloging in Publication Data
A catalogue record has been requested

ISBN 0–415–36983–5 (hbk)
ISBN 0–415–36984–3 (pbk)

Contents

Preface

Higher education has been in a 'crisis mode' for so long now that any attempt to sound the alarm one more time is apt to evoke only sighs and yawns. The modern higher educational system, particularly in the West, has survived two world wars and the Cold War, the Sixties 'cultural revolution' (which started in Berkeley, California in the early 1960s with a general rebellion against the university itself), the hyperinflation of the 1970s, and the 'political correctness' movement of the 1990s. The impact of all these batterings and shocks has been remarkably weaker than one might have anticipated. Today's typical college classroom, excluding perhaps its décor and architecture, does not look or function much differently from the way it did in the 1920s. Can one imagine any other crucial pillar of culture, or sector of the economy, that has not changed much in eighty years? It is almost impossible to imagine.

This fierce resistance to change can easily be construed, particularly by curricular traditionalists, as justification of the principle that what is time-tested is also true. But there is little evidence that higher education, particularly in the United States, is really serving its clientele, particularly when one figures the ratio of costs to benefits. Higher education has gone through various 'crises' because periodically someone, or some constituency, discovers that the expectations are absurdly far from the reality. But people stick with their existing higher educational system in the same way that a man and a woman persists in an abusive relationship. The painfully familiar seems preferable to the frighteningly unfamiliar.

This time around, however, the 'crisis' may have significant effects. The advent of digital or computer-mediated learning is not merely some kind of internal 'experiment' within the broader educational environment. It is a social, economic, and cultural shift of startling proportions from which the higher learning cannot insulate itself. As the Medieval Catholic Church carried on in much the same way for more than a millennium until the sudden intellectual and technological changes of the sixteenth century shattered its foundations, so the university as we know it has lumbered along in pretty much the same fashion – until now. It is an historical truism that the printing press and the spread of book literacy, which even from a contemporary vantage point happened for the most part overnight, made the Roman Catholic claim to exclusivity and hegemony indefensible.

Similarly, the new digital economy has already rendered the traditional 'clerical' model of post-secondary instruction untenable. A new 'Protestant' and democratic reformation of the university is now in the making. The reformation does not arise from any new kind of radical educational theory, but from the necessity of the old knowledge moving into alignment with the new order of knowledge in the digital society. Furthermore, the capacity of digital technology to change the configuration of knowledge and power in the new millennium is much greater than the printing press ever offered. In the same way that the combination of book production technology and more efficient transportation led within a generation or two in the 1500s to the coming of the 'modern' world, so digital communications and the shipping of data on a global scale must result in the emergence of what we unreservedly recognize as the 'postmodern' age. This book is as much about the shape of knowledge production in the postmodern era as it is about the institution we know as the 'university'. The book is about the new systems of knowledge creation and distribution that in effect transcends any kind of 'educational' theory or practice.

The argument in the succeeding pages is straightforward. It can be summarized as follows. First, the architecture of digital communications necessitates a new understanding of the structures and 'space' of knowledge itself. Second, this new knowledge space is consonant with the philosophical slant on the theory of representation, language, and symbolic exchange that has come to be called 'postmodernist'. Third, such knowledge may be called 'hyperknowledge', because like hyperspace in post-Newtonian cosmology it extends the directions and dimensions of knowledge *per se* in ways unanticipated even a generation ago. Fourth, the matrix for these new extensions of knowledge is what we call the 'hyperuniversity', which in no way resembles the physical university.

The philosopher Ludwig Wittgenstein once gave a famous example of what he termed a 'category mistake' in rational inquiry. The example involves a visitor to Cambridge, UK who, after being shown all the grounds and buildings, asked 'where is the university?' Wittgenstein's point, of course, was that the visitor confused the university itself, an abstract and collective entity, with the individual buildings. The visitor believed the university was an entity with a proper name, rather than a term to describe the relationship among entities we call the university. The visitor, according to Wittgenstein, had made a 'category mistake', inasmuch as he mis-applied the language of a relational totality to single, concrete existents.

Drawing on Wittgenstein's tale, however, we can go even one step farther and make the bold claim that in the not-too-distant future the same visitor may not have made a mistake after all. Or at least the visitor was well-warranted in asking the whereabouts of the univer-sity. For the particular buildings may have no special significance any longer in pulling out the connotations of the expression 'univer-sity'. The habitual association of colleges and universities with the concentration of teaching and learning into a defined and highly localized place may make no more syntactical sense than describing the location of information in 'cyberspace' with the room in which is housed a desktop computer or a server.

It is interesting that one of the earliest universities in the New World to be founded, following the establishment of Harvard on the Charles River in Cambridge, Massachusetts during the seven-teenth century, was originally intended as an early modern version of the hyperuniversity. Launched in 1701 as a democratic alternative to its counterpart in Boston, Yale University (or the 'Collegiate School', as it was initially called) was conceived as 'ambulatory, like the tabernacle in the wilderness'. The university was only nominally located in Saybrook, Connecticut, but was situated 'in various places, at the homes of the minister who gave instruction'. It was only because of the money influence of Elihu Yale, a wealthy Boston merchant, that a decision was made in 1716 to give the uni-versity a fixed 'home' in New Haven.[1]

History may becoming full circle. The increasing resistance to, or efforts to undermine hyperlearning and cybereducation, may have less to do with 'quality standards' and more with the huge amount of money and prestige invested in buildings bearing the names of

America's industrial magnates. But this time around the strangulation of the hyperuniversity in its crib may not be possible. The whole American global economy is increasingly dependent for future dynamism and growth on the digital transformation of culture. The current recession merely confirms this fact. Those corporate and academic interests that stand in the way of 'digitizing' higher education may be without realizing it attempting to retard the entire course of Western history. Higher education is the last redoubt of Medieval privilege and aristocracy. Digital learning is the true bulwark of a global democracy.

Although in recent months the arch-reactionaries of the higher learning have been pointing to the collapse of the dot.com investment bubble and the subsequent securities and accounting scandals in the United States as evidence that technology-based learning should not be trusted, the argument is both specious and inane. All social indicators show that while the technology economy in the Western world may have gone through some sizable shocks, the worldwide use of the new digital communications is steadily growing, even among the so-called electronic 'have-nots'. While expansion of the digital culture may have slowed in the developed countries, it is beginning to take off in the developing world. The digital revolution began without the aid of hucksters in the securities industry and the greed of investment bankers, and it will continue in that vein. In truth, the dependence of traditional higher learning on the largesse of the world's financial moguls will make it less, rather than more, secure in the new environment.

Acknowledgements

Portions of Chapter 2 were published as 'Digital Culture, The Third Knowledge Revolution, and the Coming of the Hyperuniversity', *Syllabus*, March, 1998. Parts of Chapter 5 were published as 'Beyond Education', *Syllabus*, November/December 1999.

For assistance in this endeavour I am indebted first of all to the University of Denver, which granted me a mini-sabbatical in the autumn of 1998 to begin this project. I would also like to acknowledge the strong support I received from the organizers of the annual *Syllabus* conferences in California and the editors of *Syllabus* magazine, who asked me to provide portions of Chapters 2 and 5 in their widely read and influential magazine. Acknowledgement is also given to my colleague Professor Jeff Rutenbeck, Director of Digital Media Studies at the University of Denver, for his partnership in curricular experimentation and stimulation of theoretical thinking along these lines; Professor Edith Wyschogrod at Rice University and Professor Charles Winquist at Syracuse University, for encouraging these musings in educational theory and postmodernist philosophy; my wife Sunny, whom I first met the very day I composed the first lines of this manuscript, and who has been a blessing ever since in all aspects of my personal life; my son Erik who has shown what today's 'digital generation' can do with the arts and humanities; our six cats whose occasional performance of 'kitten on the keys' aided me in the process of deleting verbiage that was probably worthy of excision anyway.

Chapter I

Higher education and the postmodern condition

The university is in ruins.

(Jean Baudrillard)

The university described by the French philosopher Jean Baudrillard, a doyen of today's so-called 'postmodernist' philosophy, is certainly on the eve of an enormous changeover. Regardless of whether the university is ready or prepared, it is about to embark upon the postmodern epoch. Higher education, whether it likes it or not, must respond to what the French philosopher Jean-Francois Lyotard has termed 'the postmodern condition'.

The postmodern condition is decisively the condition of living in digital times, the time of networked communications. It is what we conventionally, if not all too conveniently, call the information age, which is actually a new 'knowledge age'. It is an age when the boundaries of everything from art to philosophy to literature to economics are rinsed out, when their historical hierarchies are flattened, when their very definitions have become suspect.

What exactly do we mean by 'postmodernism'? The meaning of the term has been argued and threshed in untold popular periodicals and scholarly books and journals. It has been affiliated in the popular mind with everything from unintelligible monographs in French philosophy to trendy styles of painting and architecture to antinomian forms of belief and morality. Yet, as Hans Bertens observes in his detailed history of the concept, postmodernism is really, for better or for worst, the long-lasting intellectual legacy of the '1960s social and artistic avant-garde'. Such a sensibility is not only 'eclectic'; it is 'radically democratic'.[2]

The postmodernist revolution that began in the late 1960s was initially a cultural revolution. It was a 'youthquake', as social commentators at the time called it, that rapidly manifested itself as an intellectual pole shift. It began as a wave of Bohemian protest in the arts districts of California in the summer of 1967, exploded like a political meteor shower in the streets of Paris during May 1968, then immediately emitted a shock wave through Eastern Europe with the so-called 'Prague Spring', which would set off the tsunami that toppled the Soviet Union and international Communism not quite a generation later. Once the Berlin Wall, a lowering symbol of the divide between East and West, fell in the autumn of 1989, the way came open for the thorough transformation of the economic and social structures of those regions of the planet that were hitherto called 'capitalist' and 'socialist'.

For at least a decade theorists on both sides of the old line proclaimed the triumph of the market economy and a new golden age for the partisans of Adam Smith, as opposed to the now discredited prophets of Marx. The market indeed had replaced the inefficient, and politically repressive, command economies of the old Communist bloc and its allies. But something far more significant was boiling up beneath the surface. Whereas 'capital' in the past had signified the accumulated savings of institutions and individuals that was redeployed into new investment in technologies of production, the new global economy was coming increasingly to be driven by technological innovations that in themselves generated wealth without savings. The paradox of America's steamrollering 'capitalist' economy with a negative savings rate that showed itself in the late 1990s masked a trend that old ideologues of both left and right could not fathom or comprehend. The trend was toward the blurring of the final distinction that had defined economies, and the 'science' of economics, since the philosopher Aristotle coined the phrase *oikonomia* twenty-three hundred years ago.

That was the distinction between production and consumption, or between making and desiring. In one, slightly misleading sense, the high-tech entrepreneur from Silicon Valley in California, who once worked 150 weeks without sleeping or going home in order to sell out for a fantastic price, then recycled his or her talents into a new startup company, was a latter day parody of the now extinct, hard-working Calvinist Max Weber had described as having inadvertently created capitalism. But while Weber's capitalist exhibited a lifestyle of 'worldly asceticism' in order to accumulate the financial sources to produce more and more, the new, postmodern 'capitalist' simply engaged in feverish technological creativity while living a totally hedonistic, and in some cases, orgiastic lifestyle that he or she rarely had time to enjoy. Money in the postmodern economy no longer was a sign of privilege or control; it was an index of hyperactivity.

The university in the postmodern economy

The abolition of the proprietary and coercive ethic that had characterized the 'old economy' – capitalist as well as socialist, in other words 'industrial' – called forth an entirely different set of values that are now firmly in place for the postmodern economy. The postmodern economy is characterized by a process which the French philosopher Jean Baudrillard terms 'symbolic exchange'. In the old industrial economy, the market, and the system of exchange that accompanied it, involved manufactured things, or commodities. In the post-industrial, or postmodern, order the market is in intangible vehicles of meaning. In Baudrillard's terms the sign replaces the commodity. Contemporary cultural theorists constantly bring to our attention examples of how the new economy is 'symbolical' rather than material. Commodities are not only symbols or 'signs'; signs are also commodities.[3]

But this insight is rarely fleshed out with regard to its most important ramification – the recognition that the 'business' of knowledge within the context of what we traditionally understand as 'education' is the most important business. While the average business guru chatters on about the 'information economy' and the promise of online commerce, more discerning analysts understand that the convergence of digital technologies foreshadows an entire new way in which the human mind itself develops, and experiences the world. John Chambers, chief executive officer of Cisco Systems, manufacturer of the routers that propel data throughout the internet, has proclaimed that so-called 'e-learning' is on the verge of becoming the next frontier of internet applications. 'Education and the internet must go hand in hand', Chambers said in the autumn of 1999 during a speech before Comdex, the enormous annual gathering of computer industry manufacturers and sellers. 'It will serve as one of the great equalizers.'[4]

What will the coming of digital learning 'equalize'? Like the postmodernist revolution in thought and culture over the past twenty years, it will impart a hurricane force that reshapes the educational system as a whole. To date educators in general, and higher education in particular, have largely resisted the digital onslaught, or savvily co-opted it in a fashion that so far has absorbed its transformative energy. Teachers have replaced paper syllabi with web pages, or encouraged the use of email for out-of-class communication with the instructor. Increasingly they are employing presentation programs such as Microsoft PowerPoint with their lectures. But they have not allowed the changes in courses and classes, which the world wide web will inevitably accomplish. They have ferociously resisted the process that has taken hold by now in all other sectors of the digital society, whereby centralized management and 'top-down' authority is replaced by non-sequential and coactive networks that rely far more on the efficiency of communication than command and control.

Like the age-old Gothic cathedrals that tower over bustling European metropolises, the professoriate seeks to maintain a distinct, albeit archaic, presence amid today's 'digital kids' in the university classroom. But unlike the cathedrals, which centuries ago became historical showpieces rather than the centrepiece of town life they occupied in the late Middle Ages, the professoriate still demands pride of place. The current downswing in the financial fortunes of the high tech sector has given temporary encouragement to the Luddite factions in higher education. But the respite will be short-lived. The tension between the two worlds cannot be sustained much longer.

The obsolescence of 'teaching'

The dominant issue is not, as critics of higher education in corporate quarters continue to harp, one of educators spending too much time 'outside the classroom'. The irony is that the classroom as we know it, especially the one valued most by advocates of 'teachers doing teaching', is rapidly becoming obsolete in the emerging postmodern, digital culture. Interestingly, both conservative detractors of post-secondary learning and the guild of higher education share many of the same outworn assumptions concerning what 'instruction' is all about. The assumption is that learning remains a 'centred' activity with large numbers of students routinely focused on the teacher as well as a limited selection of carefully selected repositories of knowledge such as textbooks.

The model further presupposes that in order for instructors to instruct that they must concentrate their time and energy on a direct transmission to 'students' of what is either latent or manifest within their own favoured crania.

The postmodern prototype, on the other hand, constitutes, both a de-centred and a dispersive approach, as it does in philosophy and cultural theory, to the creation of knowledge. There is no 'body of knowledge' in the postmodern archetype; or at least it is a body, in the memorable metaphor of Gilles Deleuze and Felix Guattari, 'without organs'. That is to say, the body is not a regime of discrete functions, physiologies, and anatomical components. It is a body that remains Protean, constantly shifting in shape and deportment.

The postmodern prototype of knowledge has been a theoretical construct on both sides of the Atlantic for nearly twenty years. But it has taken the coming of digital media and the ubiquity of digital communications to incarnate within society itself the prototype. Now that the prototype pervades the social and cultural order, it will be impossible for the educational establishment to keep it at a distance. European castles, like cathedrals, continue to dot the land-scape. But their purpose as fortified structures for military defence vanished centuries ago. The 'ivory tower' also is in an analogous position to the castle of the sixteenth century. The munitions that had been developed by that period rendered it indefensible. Those countries in the sixteenth century that relied on castle defences wound up the sad victims of Europe's sanguinary wars. The same will be the case for higher education if it does not 'postmodernize', and do so quickly.

A new knowledge space

The postmodern university – or what we shall call, more technically – the 'hyperuniversity' – is an extension, and an extensive 'knowledge space', of the culture at large. What do we mean by 'knowledge space'? Pierre Lévy writes that 'once knowledge becomes the prime mover' in the world, a whole new social topography begins to emerge. 'A new anthropological space, the *knowledge space*, is being formed today, which could easily take precedence over the spaces of earth, territory, and commerce that preceded it.'[5]

The notion of knowledge space is bound up with our contempor-ary cultural understanding of space itself. Until the late nineteenth century, the concept of space suggested for the most part what the physicist Isaac Newton three hundred years before had described. Space implied a substance that underlies and supports all matter. The metaphor, of course, came from the human observation of objects in motion through air or water. Just as water buoys and sustains lighter entities, so space is the 'understructure' of everything visible and perceptible. Just as objects gliding through water displace the fluid in which they are contained, so bodies in motion dislocate the texture of space itself. This texture physicists up through the late nineteenth century named 'the ether'. And it was not until the famous Michelson–Morley experiment, designed to measure velocity of light through its 'fluid' receptacle, demonstrated the ether did not exist, that the Newtonian concept of space itself began to crumble.[6] What ensued, of course, was the theory of relativity and the revolution in scientific cosmology that came to be known as quantum physics. The so-called 'new physics' of the twentieth century advanced by Albert Einstein, Niels Bohr, and others radically redefined the meaning of the idea of space as it had been employed in both science and philosophy. For Einstein, space was now conceived as the fourth dimension, or part of the 'geometry' of space–time. Later advances in theoretical physics and mathematics redescribed space even further in non-intuitive terms.

By the same token, digital learning is radically reconstituting our intuitive, or common-sense, views of the 'space' in which education takes place. For most of the modern era the 'space' of learning has been closely associated with schools, buildings, and classrooms. Instruction is something conducted by a particular person in a particular place at a particular time. In the new universe of digital learning, on the other hand, the old 'metaphysical' notion of learning space shifts dramatically. As we shall discover, even the seemingly obvious idea that education involves teachers and students enters into question. Teaching and learning are not necessarily separate functions or professional activities, but points of co-ordination along the same spectrum. The space of the postmodern university mirrors the space of knowledge within the digital society. This space of knowledge, in turn, reflects the topology of information flows in what increasingly we recognize as a networked world.

Networks by their very nature are 'anti-hegemonic'. That is to say, they prevent the domination of any sector or region of space by a single entity, or agent. For a long while biologists believed the brain was hegemonic and hierarchical. The assumption was that 'thinking' took place in certain central or privileged portions of the brain. But brain science is rapidly realizing that human cognition depends on regularly alternating activation of different neural pathways. The internet itself is a marvellous, and actually far more intricate, simulation of the shifting patterns of electrical activity that from a physical vantagepoint amount to the phenomenon of consciousness. As most net users have been told at some time in recent years, this astounding digital communication design was developed by the military in order to protect its command and control system from destruction or disruption at vulnerable spots. In other words, the power of the internet – and its invulnerability to singular or central intervention – is based on the fact that it has no 'head', nucleus, or centre. The internet was conceived as a communications architecture that could not be sabotaged, simply because its 'ganglia', or nerve centres, cannot be localized.

Hyperspace and non-locality

The theme of 'non-locality' also pervades twentieth-century physics. In the old Newtonian picture of space and time, events were regarded as 'point-events'. That is, they could be described with mathematical precision as taking place at a certain locale at a certain exact 'point' along an axis representing what Newtonian thought called 'absolute time'. In the theoretical physics of the twentieth century, however, the presumption that change could be mapped as a transition from points A to B to C went on the fly. Physicist John Wheeler, in his cosmological model known as 'geometrodynamics', envisioned the universe Einstein had sketched as a flapping and fluctuating membrane that was constantly collapsing, reconstituting itself, and punching out 'wormholes' and 'tunnels' that connect the different regions of the space–time continuum. Particles that zoom about at the subatomic level beyond our sight are actually manifestations at particular 'locations' in space and time of waveforms that are non-local, or which paradoxically exist potentially at any time or place.

According to quantum physics, what allows us to say that a particle 'exists' at any particular site at a particular 'moment in time' is the fact that we have observed it. Observation determines location, but the unobserved still constitutes the deeper reality of the 'thing', in the same way that the magnitude of an iceberg is not visible above the surface of the ocean, or the foliage of a tuberous plant conceals the fact that growth is extensive beneath the ground.

In the technical terms of theoretical physics, we claim that the unobserved particle prior to its emergence is a 'virtual particle'. The observed particle is real.

Indeed, the analogy of tuberous growth that is latent, or potential, everywhere and overt at specific sites has become a guiding metaphor for much of postmodern thinking itself. In their landmark book *A Thousand Plateaus* Gilles Deleuze and Felix Guattari, two distinguished French writers and intellectuals who have mapped much of the discourse of postmodern thought, use the metaphor of the rhizome, the agency of such growth, to characterize the new landscape of both language and cognition. 'Any point of a rhizome can be connected to any other, and must be', they write. 'This is very different from the tree root, which plots a point, fixes an order.'[7] Unlike the tree root which anchors or 'grounds' growth (of knowledge), the rhizome 'ceaselessly establishes connections between semiotic chains'. A rhizome is 'a stream without beginning'.[8] The rhizome is the perfect biogenetic model of what in physics is described as non-locality. As Steven Best and Douglas Kellner write in their explanation of 'rhizomatics' as a root metaphor for the contemporary condition of the world: '[Rhizomatics] affirms the principles excluded from Western thought and reinterprets reality as dynamic, heterogeneous, and non-dichotomous'.[9] The heterogeneity of the real means that everything that exists is not confined within a simple concept, or assigned to a particular place. Reality itself is non-local.

The postmodern university, like the universe of twentieth-century physics, is founded on the principle of non-locality. It is also resonant with the motif of virtual and observed reality. The 'virtuality' of the postmodern university consists in the ubiquitous stock of information resources, which the digital age brings forth.

The fallacies of content

The notion that a university somehow 'contains' a singular, or proprietary, supply of what can be known, or articulated as knowledge, is no longer viable. Indeed, the vocabulary of postmodern thinking includes a phrase that can now be added to the list of pejoratives (e.g., 'racism', 'sexism', 'ageism') we use in sophisticated speech to designate a particular parochialism, prejudice, or habit of narrowmindedness. The word is 'contentism' – the misplaced preoccupation of educators, or educational administrators, with what is 'contained' within the ivy-crusted precincts of a learning facility, or inside the cinder block walls of a traditional classroom or the eight-by-eleven-and-a-half-inch page of a course syllabus. In the earlier archetype of instruction scholars 'worked' within and inhabited the geographical site recognized as a college or university. The same was true of what students did. Everything that went on 'within' a learning space corresponded to the physical space of the institution itself.

Contentism amounts to localism in thinking. Unfortunately, contentism, as a type of localism, is deeply and almost pathologically engrained in today's academic culture. The pathology runs the gamut from university presidents who insist primarily on raising money for buildings, to deans who demand that faculty hold regular 'office hours' to tenured professors who loathe the thought of reading a 'journal article' on a laptop, or off the internet, rather than in the periodicals section of a library. There is, of course, an economic motive for this sort of contentist 'fundamentalism'. During the early years of the internet executives for broadcast media (what we now call 'old media') constantly boasted about how they would gradually monopolize the internet and impose a regime of 'pay per view' in the fashion of the more exclusive forms of cable television such as Home Box Office. Their argument was that the public would demand 'content'. They were, of course, woefully wrong.

What they did not understand was that the internet itself redefined what we mean by 'content'. It has never been a question, as even so-called 'netheads' have insisted to rather silly extremes, of 'authoritarian' versus 'democratic' structures for the control and direction of information. There is always a process of editorial self-selection when information flows profusely, as has happened with the internet. The same rules for 'authorizing' or legitimating what appears as content apply to both old and new media. Branding, and brand-name recognition, apply as much to digital communications as to the older analogue communications systems. What has changed is the way in which content itself emerges. In broadcast media content was carefully crafted, shaped, assessed, and refined before it became visible, or audible, or readable.

Because there was an exceptional scarcity of communications channels, content could always be predefined by those who were the 'gatekeepers' for any particular mass audience. In the digital world such gatekeeping is impossible, though mass audiences instinctively still rely on those recognized 'sentinels' (recognized media companies, credentialled academic figures, etc.) of electronic transactions when for the most part they choose what web site to click on. In the digital era content is never pre-ordained, but is what we might call 'autochthonous' in the original sense of the Greek word. In short, it increasingly springs and grows from the 'ground' of the medium itself rather than being imported into the medium.

To be sure, there are old-style academic journals and major newspapers that still 'publish' what they have always published on the internet. But the close connection between what used to be known as 'publishing' and the creation of content has broken down. Content is now an endless 'work in process'. Digital texts are constantly undergoing revision and incorporation into documents that are in turn revised and incorporated – even in the tradition-hounded academy. The 'interactivity' that comes from the distribution of texts, or snippets of text, through email and listserves enhances this picture of things. To the degree that texts are disseminated and distributed, and that content is 'deconstrued' through infinite revisability, the university itself becomes de-localized. Professors by the very nature of the digital medium become 'independent scholars'. That does not mean that the university can dispense with scholars, or remove them from the payroll, any more than Yahoo can dispense with web designers and database programmers, or Microsoft can fire all its software engineers. It does not mean that universities as economic entities will suddenly cease to exist, anymore than Bill Gates and company will suddenly disappear from Seattle and be etherized into the Microsoft Network.

The re-spatialization of learning

But what it does signal is that education in general, and higher education in particular, must undergo a radical 're-spatialization', and to a certain extent, a re-temporalization, of its familiar enterprise. This re-spatialization is urged onward by the digital economy itself. It is not so much, as Marshall McLuhan argued some time back, that the 'medium is the message', but the medium now becomes the 'mediator' of the messages that coalesce into what we regard as a society's 'knowledge base'.

As Werner Kelber has astutely noted, the philosophical or 'epistemological' transitions of Western culture, which we know as by such labels as 'Platonism' or 'Scholasticism', and which commenced with Socrates' band of disciples in ancient Athens and continued up through the high Middle Ages and the Protestant Reformation of the sixteenth century, are rooted in synchronous changes of communications media. Western philosophy as a whole, which was founded on the method of critical argumentation the Greeks named 'dialectics', would not have arisen if writing had not replaced recitation and oral memorization as the dominant type of intellectual culture. Thomas Aquinas would not have been possible without the spread of monasteries and the explosion of 'scribalism', involving the copying of specialized texts and their circulation among clerical elites. Protestantism as a form of religious democracy, and the later secular democratic movements of later centuries, as all students of modern history recognize, was occasioned by Gutenberg's invention of the printing press.[10]

In subsequent pages we will explore how the postmodern university promises to unfold in accordance with already recognized patterns of historical and social change. The guiding precept for this change, at the same time, is fairly straightforward. In the same way that a 'house is not a home', as the old saying runs, a college or university is no longer a school. The postmodern university is instead *a knowledge and research emporium* – a multi-centred, if not in fact centreless, learning 'centre' that is radically de-centralized. The digital epoch is at once the age of distributed learning, wherein communication takes precedence over content, inquiry is prior to instruction, results rule over the rules. The postmodern university follows the 'diagram' of the postmodern economy, which is no longer one of industrial manufacturing. Just as the industrial economy in the nineteenth century re-organized the village craft economies by centralizing production in one locale and creating regimented and specialized job functions, so the 'modern university' evolved about the same time, by aping Prussian models of military organization, what has come to be known, without even the benefit of similitude, as a 'knowledge factory'. But both the postmodern economy and the postmodern university are built on a different sort of organizational scaffolding. It is an economy of mobile capital, mobile work forces, and mobile or 'just-in-time' inventory and distribution systems. Such mobility depends on de-spatialization as well as what Deleuze and Guattari term 'de-territorialization'. Quoting the architect Charles Jencks, who coined the term 'postmodernism', this new organizational anatomy powers 'an economy that is more flexible and creative any one based simply on the Modernist and Fordist model'.[11] The knowledge map of the digital terrain is not the same as the territory, principally because the territory has been de-terroritialized. It has to a wide extent been made 'virtual'.

The kind of learning that takes place in this environment is no longer learning as we know it. The university is no longer the university as we know it. Everything is extended. We are witnessing the advent of the hyperuniversity.

Chapter 2

The third knowledge revolution and the coming of the hyperuniversity

> We live in a moment of history where change is so speeded up that we begin to see the present only when it is already disappearing.
>
> (R. D. Laing)

So much of the pedagogical debate these days centres on what can, cannot, should, or should not, be done with computers in the classroom. But computer-based instruction and inquiry is simply the driveshaft that turns a broader, and more diffuse, revolution now underway across the spectrum of post-secondary learning. We will denote these present sea changes as the 'third knowledge revolution'.

By the third knowledge revolution we mean the movement from knowledge that depends on a centrally located 'manufacturing' system to knowledge as a global and consumer-driven process of active inquiry, exploration, and interaction. This revolution has been ignited by the advent of online computing, but its significance goes far beyond the explosive growth of online computing.

The first knowledge revolution was the beginning and use of language. The second knowledge revolution, of course, took place more than four millennia ago with the invention of writing. Writing, as the rise of the Oriental city-states shows, allowed for the aggregation of tribes and villages into urban complexes through the apparatus of royal administration. The ancient, oral legacies of rural communities, vested in story-tellers and shamans, retreated.

As both information and communication became the property of court functionaries and 'scribal' bureaucracies, knowledge was transformed into the mode with which we have been chiefly familiar for many thousands of years – an expanding, but essentially controlled, repository of standardized, as well as 'canonized', methods, facts, and concepts. It was this standardization of the forms of knowledge that became the ballast of what we call 'civilization'.

The third knowledge revolution is now in full swing. Although the college or university long ago supplanted the imperial palace as the site for 'scholarly' labour, and the telecommunications revolution that commenced after World War II challenged dramatically à la McLuhan the regime of print culture, it has only been with the advent of easily accessible public computer networks that we can discern the first glintings of this new revolution.

Fads in instruction come and go. In the past three decades the pendulum of 'curricular reform' has swung back and forth between professionalism and the liberal arts, between political liberalism and conservatism, between generalism and specialism, between technological enthusiasm and a kind of anti-technological fundamentalism. But the underlying template for the nurturing and delivery has not changed significantly, because the basic social archetype of knowledge has not really changed, until quite recently.

The most common phrase that metaphorically describes what has gone on in post-secondary education for many years is 'the production of knowledge'. The locution has been intoned repeatedly throughout the twentieth century in college catalogues, tenure review guidelines, and development office brochures. Although this expression has its origins in the high industrial age of the nineteenth century and conveys a self-awareness that harks all the way back to Hammurabi, it characterizes for the most part what still defines the Western university at the close of the millennium.

Contrary to the conventional twentieth-century wisdom, knowledge does not substantially change as technology changes. The 'scientific revolution' of the modern era was not so much a byproduct of economic and technological advances as it was the fruition of the religious and ideological upheavals of the sixtieth and early seventeenth centuries.

The scientific revolution did not, as we are accustomed to believing, constitute an underlying shift in the nature of knowledge. It was instead a 'revolution' that installed a new hierarchy for the 'authorization' of knowledge. It deposed the theologian and enthroned the experimental philosopher. Bacon's *Novum Organon* and Descartes' *Discourse on Method* are the critical texts in the history of thought that exemplify this transformation.

The nature of knowledge is alchemized when the social infrastructure for the allocation of knowledge is modified radically.

A metamorphosis in the nature of knowledge, in turn, affects the institutions in which knowledge is housed, processed, and distributed. Such change is what we mean by a 'knowledge revolution'.

When writing was fabricated at the dawn of civilization, chiefly for the purpose of record-keeping, a fundamental change in the makeup of communicative action ensued as well. Signification was no longer for the most part interpersonal, but public in its effect and scope. We can surmise that writing itself through the spread of literacy helped foster the political notion of the *res publica*. The democratic ideal of a literate, if not a learned, public has its genesis in the social capacities of literacy *per se*.

Writing engendered the second knowledge revolution, because no longer were teaching and learning something 'esoteric'. Conceptual, as opposed to practical, understanding was now possible on a grand scale. Knowledge could be churned out, not just steeped and mellowed.

Similarly, the coming of so-called 'computer mediated communications' that rely on digitized representations that can be disseminated easily and cheaply over integrated, 'dialup', global, public networks – the technical description of what is conventionally known as 'the internet' – are rapidly and ineluctably reshaping our prototypes of what it means to 'know' something.

Prior to the digitization of communications, knowledge – or at least theoretical knowledge, which is what we really have in mind – could only be stored and 'shepherded' by guild-trained 'experts' with the power to make decisions about what could be passed on to the public through far-flung distribution channels. The self-published book or pamphlet, the 'free university' course, or the private, promotional video were not terribly difficult, or expensive, to concoct. But the costs of, and technological barriers to, simple, mass distribution were always daunting. Certified authorities determined what justified economically the distribution of a given 'knowledge product'.

In the digital universe, however, what we term 'knowledge' is self-selecting. It is true that so much of what can be found at any curve, curbside, or offramp to the so-called 'information superhighway' is pedestrian, silly, ill informed, or plainly uninteresting. But conversely that does not mean the public requires highly trained and specialized 'mediators', as academic and broadcast media critics of the internet are wont to remind us, to 'show them the way' to the heavenly city of approved wisdom.

Most of what one hears or comes across in a given day at the office, on the radio, in the newspaper, or in casual conversation is not what we call 'knowledge' in the lofty sense of the word. But, for that matter, neither is what one acquires from other students in a classroom, what is discussed in a college dormitory, or even what is often picked by professors as 'social data' for study and reflection – e.g., political speeches, lyrics of pop music, statistical surveys.

The common complaint of academic specialists that the internet is of no use because it is rife with uncredentialled yammering, prejudice camouflaged as discussion, not to mention intellectual trash, makes about as much sense as grousing that one should not pay attention to anything anyone says outside a lecture hall. What such specialists beneath their pious protestations really mean is that they are offended anybody can have access to what anybody has to say.

The borderline between 'knowledge' and 'information' in common, as opposed to privileged, usage is more subtle than we realize. In actual practice the dividing line is little more than what certain individuals, or communities of individuals that call themselves professional 'peers', deem to be the proper means of interpreting, stylizing, representing, reconstructing, rendering, or criticizing what is said, or signified, in the public domain.

In the common era we may designate A.D. ('after digitization'). The Platonic dualism of 'opinion' and 'truth' has always held the academy in a kind of unsuspecting, and unself-conscious, bewitchment, and it is usually the subtext for any distinction between so-called 'information' and would-be 'knowledge'. And, as was the case for the Platonists, knowledge is strictly 'academic', information is the common sense of the populace.

So long as the guilds could effectively guard the gateways to 'information', the question of knowledge was for the most part moot. But the web page has been more devastating in collapsing the walled cities of truth than the artillery of the sixteenth century that made the baron's castle indefensible. The impact to date has been greater in journalism than in the halls of ivy. Journalists can no longer manage the news so easily by closeting their 'sources'.

The sources are promiscuously available to the public at large. Witness the mass deaths of the Heaven's Gate cult. Virtually everything reporters wrote about the group came at some point from the internet. And the same trend is already evident with scholarly 'publishing'.

But the loss of elite 'authority' is not even as telling for the new intellectual landscape wrought by the third knowledge revolution as the shattering of disciplinary boundaries. As Michel Foucault noted almost a generation ago, the disciplinary approach is a late modernist obsession. Just as the enclosure of the commons to create agribusiness was a necessary prelude to the mass production economy and the mobilization of wage labour in England, so the disciplinary frenzy that began with the Prussians' state university during the second half of the nineteenth century foreshadowed the 'industrialization' of knowledge that culminated in the American research university.

Strict disciplinarity, on the other hand, is impossible in a networked world. Furthermore, the routes by which one pursues knowledge on the 'net' through hypertext links creates a new topography of study and reflection that Lewis Perelman has dubbed 'hyperlearning'. Perelman sketched his manifesto for hyperlearning in his book *School's Out* published in 1992. Perelman begins with a sort of oracular pronouncement that calls into question many of the presuppositions of technology-related 'educational theory':

> This book is not about education. It is about an economic transformation that is being driven by an implacable technological revolution. It is not about saving schools, or improving schools, or reforming schools, or even reinventing schools – it's about removing altogether the increasingly costly barrier schooling poses to economic and social progress.[12]

In the book Perelman describes a 'new generation of technology [that] has blown the social role of learning completely inside out'. Learning is no longer an immediate function of the conventional profession and placeholder of learning that we call 'education', or 'schooling'. No longer confined to the 'box of a school classroom', learning is something that 'permeates every form of social activity – work, entertainment, home life – outside of school'.[13] Hyperlearning represents the fusion of both teaching and learning. In the distant, and not-too-distant past, learning was wholly dependent on the mediation, or intervention, of learning specialists who toiled within a specially built and hierarchically controlled learning infrastructure we know as the 'educational world'. But in the culture of hyperlearning the educational world is replaced by what Perelman dubs the 'telecosm' – a new, communications-based environment that 'makes all knowledge accessible to anyone, anywhere, any-time'.[14]

According to Peter Denning, the coming 'virtual university' will be infused with hyperlearning. 'The supporting technologies fit hyper-learning, a non-linear model of learning', says Denning, emphasizing active exploration over passive acquisition, project completion over course accreditation. Denning contrasts the traditional course with the one designed, according to the principles of hyperlearning. Denning characterizes a 'traditional course' as 'a series of lectures, held in classrooms at weekly intervals, with homework practice in between'. In the traditional course everyone follows the same regi-men and pace. But Denning exhorts us to 'imagine a new model', which is essentially a 'learning room' where people come and go at their own volition, or the discretion of the room manager. The teacher does not hold sway over the classroom as much as 'offer guidance' to those who may have failed to navigate their way suffi-ciently. 'Hyperlearning' here is used in the sense of the ability of the learner 'to jump to other dimensions', as is the case when a mathe-matician speaks of 'hyperspace', or when in literature we invoke the term 'hypertext'.[15]

The rule of instruction 'anytime, anywhere', which is the hallmark of the new online Western Governors University, follows this non-linear pattern. Although the WGU was originally set up as a multi-state consortial arrangement to support and finance 'distance education' on a larger scale than ever envisioned, its guiding philo-sophy increasingly has been configured, if not quite wittingly, by the hyperlearning model. Distance learning experiments were not a serious threat to traditional higher education prior to the explosion of public, digital networks, inasmuch as they offered only an elec-tronic semblance of the regular classroom without any fundamental retooling of the pedagogical apparatus. Their selling point was 'convenience', which came at the expense of interactivity.

Network-based instruction, however, once the full capabilities of the new technology dawns on educational providers, will transform the academic environment in such a way that the relationship, and most likely the ratio, between teaching and learning becomes far more pronounced than in the past. Network-based instruction, if implemented correctly, promises to show serious gains in classroom efficiencies with regard to the assessment of curricular objectives and outcomes.

Education as an 'industry' may finally begin to demonstrate increased productivity in the manner that its political constituencies demand, much in the same way that American business after a decade, or more, of false starts finally began in the early 1990s to exhibit new and dramatic economies resulting from automation and investment in technology. In contrast to the usual anxieties of knowledge professionals, however, the move to 'hyperclassrooms' and 'hypercourses' does not at all mean a reduction in the value, or employability, of faculty. Hypercourses will change the role, not to mention the routines, of academic personnel significantly to the extent that they blur the entrenched, and for the most part indecipherable, distinction between 'teaching' and 'research'. We call this new phenomenon in whatever precise form it takes the 'hyperuniversity'.

Former Colorado Governor Roy Romer, who helped shape the vision behind WGU, has outlined what he saw as the new faculty 'job description'. Teaching at WGU means that an instructor might tell their students that 'from now on you're going to get your information through technology, through the Internet or through CD-ROMs. And we'll take the same approach to building your skill levels'. As a result, the professor will spend more time involved in aiding the student with critical thinking, problem-solving, communication, and group involvement.[16] The WGU plan, of course, assumes an independent and responsible adult learner who knows what he or she wants, can be easily prompted to select tasks and carry through with them, and is not in need of the intense 'socialization' that a traditional campus education provides. Nonetheless, the push toward 'client-centred' and 'active' learning which the new, digitally hip, 'university without walls' epitomizes is the deeper and surging trend within all of education.

Psychological and demographic studies of the young, 'wired' generation increasingly make it obvious that internet 'surfing' with its focus on self-directed information gathering and response is not just an idle, adolescent pastime, but represents a bedrock change in the motivational and cognitive makeup of an entire segment of society. This segment is close to entering college *en masse*. Whether 18-year-olds are mature enough to decide what they want to learn, and how to do it, is not as relevant on the surface as it may seem. The point is that the learning styles and orientation of the primary college customer are swinging 180 degrees because of the online revolution. Even if adolescents are not capable of deciding what is best for them as far as educational goals are concerned, they certainly will be far better positioned to choose how they want to proceed toward those goals.

The elimination of 'contact hours' and 'seat time' as the measure of academic progress, which the WGU foresees, will inevitably compel students to take more responsibility for their education, not less. According to Alfred Bork, 'the key to success is that we must determine, on a moment-to-moment basis, just what the student knows and just what learning problems are occurring, so that explicitly tailored help can be made available'. The crucial factor is not the intervention of new technologies but the new configurations of intellectual discovery that these technologies bring forth. 'New ways of learning allow new learning structures. I do not say "courses" because in a full self-paced distance environment, learning will be a continuous process from birth to death.' In this new context 'learning and evaluation' are no longer separate from each other, but are 'intimately blended'.[17] Faculty who shake their heads and cluck over the proposition that students do need to be told what courses to take, when to take them, and how precisely to take them should remember that up until the mid-Sixties most colleges considered it almost an eternal verity that sexual behaviour in dormitories should be tightly regulated by the institution.

That presumption was blown away with a hurricane of social change in less than a year. In the late Nineties the principle of *in loco parentis* remains just as fragile, except that now it may apply to the curriculum. The eventual layout of the hyperuniversity will be a function of what might be called the cultural *episteme* (Foucault's term) ensuing from the third knowledge revolution. All we can predict at this point is that the old 'knowledge factories' embodied in the 'comprehensive university' of the twentieth century are on the verge of obsolescence. The question is not whether the university is going to have to change dramatically in the next five years. The question is simply whether it can change.

In recent years many apocalyptic voices, from management guru Peter Drucker to celebrated author George Gilder, to New York University professor Eli Noam, and even to some of the leaders of *Educom*, the prestigious national organization that deals with trends in educational technology, prophesied 'the end of the university'.[18] These voices are often perceived as voices in the wilderness. The educational eschaton may not be as closely at hand as many have lately imagined. In fact, both the overpromise of technology by itself and the tenacity of the educational establishment in the aftermath of the 'roaring Nineties' are evident. But we can still project the following scenarios based on a comparison of the second and third knowledge revolutions to give us some sense of how the hyperuniversity might be used to 'harness' its energies (see Table 2.1).

This typology to be sure is artificial. Paradigm shifts are never total. The old persists into the new, and the new is anticipated in the old. The issue is one of dominance and emphasis. Campus education is to the present decade what ocean liners were to the

Table 2.1

	Traditional knowledge paradigm	Emerging knowledge revolution
Nature of knowledge production	Centralized, 'institutional'	De-centralized, personalized
Character of learning	Top-down, authoritarian, regimented, content-defined	Bottom-up, client-centred, outcomes-designed, task-oriented
Structures of education	Provider controlled, guild-based, campus-centred	Customer-driven, standards-related, communications-centred
Knowledge acquisition	Formal instruction, degree programmes with uniformly defined courses, inculcation of peer-developed content	Self-directed inquiry, certification programmes built around specific objectives, 'menu-driven' selection of curricular options
Knowledge space	Institutionally concentrated, administered by 'docents', aristocratic	Socially distributed, gated by access technologies, democratic
Criteria for 'expertise'	Length of formal education, degree of specialization, affiliation with institutions and professional societies	Application of formal education to social knowledge, interdisciplinary facility, participation in broad, cultural 'knowledge base'

1940s, when air transportation began to capture the market for transoceanic travel. In 1945 most journeys across the seas were in luxury boats. In 1955 they were by airplane. The great liners did not disappear after 1950, however. They merely became the special 'pleasure' of the wealthy. Less prestigious vessels turned to carrying non-human cargo.

The same will be true for a high-priced, campus educational experience. The most prestigious of the 'luxury liners' (e.g., Harvard, Stanford, Swarthmore) will inevitably survive. The middling ones will go the way of the 'merchant' ships of that period. In his essay 'Everybody Else's College Education', Louis Menand has also declared the 'end' of the traditional college education, and the traditional college professor.[19] His argument, however, is more subtle and persuasive than many of the Tofflerian techno-determinists. Menand points out that since the turn of the century the reference group for all of higher education has been the elite, campus schools. That referencing was sustainable so long as state colleges and universities, in which the vast majority of American students are educated, had plenty of money and there was no political pressure to the contrary. Menand suggests that as state-supported learning veers in an entirely different direction, as we can see in the case of WGU, the whole culture of higher education will be transmuted. It is the airplanes versus ships rationale.

Thus we can probably expect that the hyperuniversity itself will also be distinguished from the traditional university along the following lines (see Table 2.2).

No one really means to suggest that one day soon all traditional universities will vanish from the face of the earth and completely new types of educational approaches will pop up all over the place. The third knowledge revolution is forcing an organizational upheaval all across the board, and the higher learning is not immune. The concept of the hyperuniversity betokens less a predicted, new educational entity than, in the words of the famous sociologist Max Weber, an 'ideal type' of revised delivery structure and corporate culture that will surely implant itself in traditional institutions in many instances, and flourish de novo in others.

In addition, the hyperuniversity should be set apart theoretically from the ever popular idea of converting education into a 'business' that continues to captivate private industry and some radical reformers. Proprietary education is not new, and the potential of the new information technologies to foment extramural learning

Table 2.2

	Traditional university	Hyperuniversity
Instructional pattern	Course credits, class schedules, contact hours	Competency exams, tutorials, certification
Classroom formats	Instructor meets same group of students during class period, courses held at 'central campus'	Instructor interacts with students over networks and face-to-face at *ad hoc* times and places, courses 'online' and at various locations
Administrative structure	Universities divided into schools and departments, which reflect divisional specialties, and programmes	Universities built around 'pathways of study' and certification programmes, faculty clustered in 'learning centres' and professional groups, as in medical and law practice
Student life	Baccalaureate and graduate degrees with majors and minors, residency or commuter campuses, student services geared to physical concentration of enrollees	Competency-related degrees and certification programmes, 'hypercampuses' that make attendance in physical classrooms less frequent as well as crucial, increasing integration of school with the workplace
Economic structure	Income mostly from credit-hour tuition and sponsored research in large schools	Income from flat-rate, modular charges for degree progress and information industry 'entrepreneurship'

strategies has led many business pundits to the false conclusion that learning as a whole can be commercialized. The non-profit nature of education, nurtured by thousands of years of clerical traditions and idealistic values, militates against the business model. Although education, like churches, today has adopted many administrative, marketing, and 'bottom-line' standards that make it function like a business, the pure profit motive will always remain incompatible with the social aims of effective education.

Nor should it be confused with 'distance learning'. Although distance learning constituencies have been pivotal in pushing hyperlearning models, such as WGU, there is growing evidence that the baseline concept of 'remote education', or contemptuously 'couch potato education', by itself is simply not that appealing to the majority of consumers. An explanation may lie simply in the product concept in most people's minds of what constitutes learning.

Distance education is to education what mobile homes are to homes. Specific people buy mobile homes under specific circumstances, and the market for such homes has always, and slowly, been expanding. But the mobile home does not, and will never, comport with the average home buyer's sentiment of the home as a permanent, well-crafted, and comfortable edifice built on one's own private land. By the same token, a 'campus' education will remain the dream of parents for their children, if not for middle-aged adults who have 'retreaded'.

The hyperuniversity will employ what are obviously perceived as 'distance learning' modalities to project the range and reach of the new hyperuniversity. Just as very few people buy homes any more that have been built without any prefabricated or modular construction methods, so few educational consumers in the next twenty years will be able to afford what William Massy and Robert Zemsky have called 'handicraft learning' à la the cosy, completely residential liberal arts college.

> Universities that succeed in the market will, like large suburban residential developers, have preserved the 'feel' of ivied halls while strongly satisfying the kinds of consumer desires which are transforming the whole of education. These desires include class and schedule flexibility, workplace relevance, outcomes-designed learning, and adult 'home schooling' (when necessary).[20]

There is no way the third knowledge revolution can fail to rattle the jalousies of the higher learning. Saying it will have little impact, and that affairs will continue as normal, is not much different from saying that the invention of the internal combustion engine did not affect transportation. Indeed, the hyperuniversity of tomorrow will probably be the benchmark for what people normally imagine as the 'university' itself. In the wired institutions of the new century the digital interface between mind and machine will constitute a whole new kind of intellectual stretch. But it will seem as regular and routine as today's lectures and book assignments. Computers will no longer be add-ons, or prosthetic innovations. As Robert Heterick and John Gehl note, '[technological] systems won't be tools anymore; they will simply be the environment'.[21]

Chapter 3

From medieval caravan to information superhighway

Toward a new epistemology of learning

> I do not fear computers. I fear lack of them.
>
> (Isaac Asimov)

What kind of educational 'experience' occurs when we introduce computers into the classroom? The tally is only beginning to come in with regard to what we call the 'effectiveness' of student learning in the new computer-mediated environment; but there is one thing we know for certain. The era of digital technology is rapidly producing an entirely new, and uncharted, terrain of cognition and human sensibility.

In the late nineteenth century, German philosophers coined the term *Lebenswelt* ('life world') to characterize the enveloping and complex set of occasions out of which knowledge arises. For millennia the life world was primarily a universe of face-to-face interactions augmented and enhanced by evolving systems of written communication. With the advent of broadcast radio and television the simulation of face-to-face (or voice-to-voice) response made the life world even more intricate, though the social consensus always registered a suspicion of the kind of political regime fostered through such means of simulation. We have only to call to mind the now archetypal Big Brother in George Orwell's *1984* to recognize the problematic character of every 'telepolis' and the way in which any fabrication of face-to-face relations is perceived somehow as dehumanizing. For many today the same assumption holds concerning the kinds of exchanges that take place in cyberspace, or as 'virtual reality'. If one cannot, at least in theory, smell the breath of our interlocutors, the possibilities of manipulation are magnified.

In educational debates this suspicion plays out with regard to the debates over 'residential' versus 'distance' education. The residential learning experience is still prized by most educators over the new cybermodalities because of the presupposition that intersubjective kinds of instruction are somehow intrinsically more valuable. Never mind that quantitative research is beginning to show that students actually learn more, and learn it more rapidly, when they are compelled to work in a 'virtual classroom'.[22] The prejudice in favour of the face-to-face is emblazoned throughout our educational landscape, and goes a long way toward explaining the notorious inefficiency and 'unreformability' of the American educational system from kindergarten through graduate school. So much of what we esteem about education, however, has little to do with instruction. Instead it has to do with the preservation of the traditional American social matrix for learning, as illustrated by the sovereignty of high school and college football. The myth of residential learning is sustained by empirical evidence that students in general, and younger students in particular, feel more comfortable and less 'alienated' if they have green, Edenic campuses through which to amble daily. But the truth is that socialization and education are not necessarily one and the same, although no one would argue that the former can be excised entirely, or anywhere near in its entirety, from the learning process.

The digital revolution, however, may be changing all that. As Neal Brodsky argues, colleges and universities are about to be beset by a 'new generation of learners' whose skills and expectations derive from growing up 'on the net'. The 'approaching college generation', he says, 'is partially rooted in the neural-quick satisfaction of seeing JAVA applets and hearing WAV files at the touch of a keystroke'.[23] We are quite familiar with the kinds of software functions and applications with which a net-savvy student is generally acquainted. But the notion of 'neural-quick satisfaction' suggests an unprecedented type of epistemology that undergirds the learning experience.[24]

Digital learning anchored in a new epistemology

The view that all theories of learning must be anchored in an epistemology, or a theory of knowledge, has generally been ignored by educational pundits in the past generation. The more essential features of the intellectual adventure has seemed trifling to them. In true pragmatist fashion, American educational writers have emphasized the 'goals' and 'outcomes' of instruction. The entire educational reform wave that began to burgeon in the early 1980s and crested about ten years later was founded almost exclusively on this tactic for dealing with the issue. But meanwhile a dramatic and qualitative change in what had already been surveyed was in the making. The change can largely be described as *a shift from receptive to active learning*. The push for 'active learning' predates the introduction of computers into the instructional arena. Indeed, the term became something of a buzzword toward the end of the educational reform wave in the early 1990s, though a clear application and specificity was always lacking.

The premise of active learning is so simple it boggles thought. It implies that learning, or teaching for that matter, is optimized whenever the inquiring mind is turned loose on a set of tasks or aims, rather than simply loading the brain with a carload of prefabricated materials. The ideal of active learning has always been a sore point for what we might call the American educational magisterium – the guild of teachers and curricular overseers at all levels who are, for the most 'content specialists' rather than instructional artisans. Active learning means that content cannot be easily filtered, edited, and reprocessed through the academic control system the magisterium establishes.[25]

It is for this reason that the revolution in computer-mediated schooling is not likely to be as bloodless as many would want, or anticipate. The threat to traditional learning, as well as the psychological and ideological resistance that is likely to become fierce in a few short years, does not stem mainly from the technology *per se*. It arises from the manner in which what broadly can be termed 'scholarship' is radically altered. In the computer-mediated setting the hierarchical, top-down distribution of increasingly mediated knowledge is turned topsy-turvy. Mediation by the 'machine' paradoxically leads to an unmediated relationship between the learner and all that is learned.

This phenomenon is most pronounced in the use of the internet as a 'virtual' library and classroom. Traditionalists rightly complain it is folly to turn students loose on the world wide web because there is no criterion of 'selection' or discrimination among the myriad sites and links that they might encounter in the use of a particular search engine. But this complaint also conceals a fear that the students might learn something that does not have prior 'authorization' from them. It is true that students can find anything they want

on the web, but the same is true if they go to a public library. What
the traditionalists are really saying is that it is much easier in the era
of the internet for students to learn on their own, and that anxiety
comes readily to be translated into a condemnation of the ease of
access rather than to facing up to the genuine challenge – the
question of authority.

access to info doesn't equal learning

Teaching discrimination in content

Of course, teachers can teach students how to utilize the same principles of discrimination in telling whether a particular document
should be given serious consideration, or to what degree it contains
misinformation and errors. For example, one of the most hackneyed
objections by anti-net factions within the academy is the observation
that the web is populated with pages by various racists, anti-Semites,
not to mention 'holocaust denial' hacks. The argument is simply a
more sophisticated variant on the complaint of Christian fundamen-
talist parents that the internet is nothing but a sink of pornography.
The suggestion is that students might be influenced by these sites, if
they found them, and would not be able to tell the difference
between poisonous propaganda and intelligent argument.

Such a prospect, as it turns out, is specious. Ordinary people
encounter the same kind of pseudo-intellectual offal in their daily
comings and goings, and are rarely persuaded. If they are properly
educated, or trained in critical thinking, in the first place, the
danger evaporates. The only difference is that the web allows all
kinds of information, particularly textual information, to congregate
under the same umbrella. The pedagogical presumption is that
students cannot tell the difference. That presumption requires
examination. *un-backed up assertion*

The most tantalizing question to emerge from recent educational
research is exactly why students learn more effectively with computer mediation. The answer will probably never spring forth
directly from the repositories of empirical research and data. But if
we map out the epistemology of the new learning in careful fashion
we may begin to achieve an idea.

Defining the new epistemology

The epistemology of the new learning can be contrasted with that
of the old. At the same time, we must keep in mind that learning

epistemologies are never isolated from the cultural milieux of their time. In other words, paradigms of learning go hand in glove with paradigms of knowledge. If we are, almost by definition, in a 'paradigm shift', as Thomas Kuhn has called it, we are witnessing both a change in the knowledge and the learning paradigm. We have seen how the current 'knowledge revolution' implies a new model of the knowledge business itself. But it is still necessary to follow through with a micro-analysis of how knowledge itself emerges from the new learning process that attends the current revolution.

The former epistemology of learning, as we have indicated, was founded upon the premise that knowledge is somehow pre-existent and is transmitted, like a radio signal, from instructor to student. If learning does not take place, it is either because the instructor is incompetent, the student is not motivated or capable, or somehow there is a breakdown in the communication channel between what in information theory we call 'sender' and 'receiver'. But the key proposition is that the maximum amount of knowledge is contained in the original 'message' and either reaches the recipient intact, or degrades over time. This prototype, in fact, coincides broadly with the dominant picture of knowledge that has pervaded all Western philosophy since the Middle Ages. In the philosophical literature it is known as 'metaphysical realism'. In the modern context it is what we call 'naïve empiricism'.

The doctrine of metaphysical realism necessarily entails a mediating authority. That is because knowledge received is always subject to distortion, and people throughout the ages have naturally made the inference that the distortion can be prevented, or at least diminished, by allowing for some privileged interpreter of what is communicated between the source and the recipient. There was a time in the seventeenth and eighteenth centuries when philosophers believed that the average person could know whatever is ultimately knowable. But that 'democratic' point of view gave way a century later to the position that even a common-sense understanding may be misguided. Advanced 'scientific' epistemologies replaced popular wisdom. Experts of various stripes now reigned where natural knowledge was once regarded as authoritative in its own right.

The ideals of American education were originally democratic and naturalistic – 'Jeffersonian' as we like to call them. The idyll of the one-room schoolhouse in which the nation's great statesmen and leaders were nurtured embodies this prescript. But in the late nineteenth century the German and covertly anti-democratic model of a highly organized, hierarchical structure with a vertical chain of command where knowledge flowed from top to bottom, as in a great army, gained currency. The new system was useful for educating masses of immigrants with no prior socialization in the American way of life. And it was relatively cost-efficient. It engendered the current concept of learning as something that takes place within an educational 'system'.

The new paradigm is rooted in the American experience

The new paradigm of learner-driven, or client-centred, education has its genesis, on the other hand, in American history and American experience. The sentiment can be summed up in the dictum of John Dewey, who is probably America's most distinguished philosopher of education. In fact, it was Dewey who commented that philosophy itself is the 'general theory' of education. Though Dewey has been excoriated by conservatives each generation for having undermined discipline and standards with his alleged prescriptions for 'progressive education', the foolishness and laxity in which pedagogical test-marketers have indulged themselves at different times has less to do with the application of Dewey's ideas themselves than with wrong-headed thinking in general about education. Dewey's approach can be summed up in a few simple propositions.

- *Proposition 1.* All learning is essentially task-defined and goal-directed.
- *Proposition 2.* Pedagogical strategy and instructional design must be geared toward maximizing the student's abilities to accomplish those tasks and reach those goals.
- *Proposition 3.* There is always a 'feedback' loop to learning in the sense that the experienced gained in labouring toward certain aims helps give a clearer picture of those objectives themselves.

There is a general misconception, of course, that client-centred learning inevitably makes the student into a 'customer', who then has the right to demand anything he or she wants, at whatever price he or she stipulates.

While competition for bodies to fill classroom space may have pushed education in general, and higher education in particular, in this direction over the last twenty years, the trend has not resulted from deployment of client-centred learning tactics. The opposite is the case. So much of educational administration at all levels has focused on strategies of seat-warming (in the K-12 environment that has meant ever more elaborate protocols for baby-sitting. In higher education it is summed up in the peculiar and elusive notion of student 'recruitment and retention'). The obsession with seat-warming is a chronic and increasingly systemic disease of an increasingly obsolete 'militarized' educational administration model. Command systems of learning, however, work no more effectively than command economies. Client-centred learning is nothing more than the introduction of 'market economics' into the educational equation. The truth is that most people, even wanton adolescents, seek credible degrees. When goals are firmly stated, the means to attain those goals are given in abundance, and structures of performance assessment are genuinely in place, learning will happen.

Client-centred, or learner-based, learning is the natural output of computer-mediated instruction. Indeed, it is the most predictable outcome. Trying to impose a regime of computer instruction on the traditional, lecture-centred, 'sage-on-the-stage' style of classroom is like outfitting a pull cart with wings, aerons, and a jet engine. It can be done, but the product is strange, monstrous, and inappropriate to its real use. That, in fact, may be one of the main reasons why the 'digitization' of contemporary society and the workplace has not been matched by comparable structural changes in education. What has been done by and large is not entirely serviceable.

As Warren Baker, Thomas Hale, and Bernard R. Gifford point out:

> Despite the effectiveness of CMI materials relatively little use is made of technology in mainstream college teaching. Whole-class, lock-step synchronous teaching continues as the predominant teaching method, particularly in entry-level courses in mathematics, the basic sciences and engineering. Not even the National Research Council's (NRC) periodic pleas that greater use be made of technology to meet the learning assistance needs of an increasingly diverse student population, has succeeded in reducing higher education's reliance upon conventional teaching methods.[26]

Traditional learning is controlled learning

The reason conventional teaching methods persist, despite evidence they are not necessarily that effective, is that they warrant and preserve a type of educational experience that flows from the 'controller' – in this instance, the classroom teacher with all his or her inherent know-how. Contrast this kind of carefully regulated learning ambience with the 'open road' that is, in theory at least, the 'information superhighway'. In the computer-mediated setting the learner has a limited set of ends and a vast array of means. The labyrinth of hypertexts and hyperlinks that make up the world wide web offers an expansive medley of possible trajectories of information and analysis to explore. The mixing of so-called 'asynchronous' modalities with synchronous and interactive forms of technology, such as chat and when available video conferencing, makes the blend even richer.

The criticism of web-based learning that it offers no 'guidance' to the learner is only partially valid. No self-respecting pedagogue would simply turn his or her students loose on the information superhighway any more than they would merely tell them to go to a library and learn everything they could about management, or calculus, or art history. The guidance itself comes from the contours of the system, and how the pedagogical architect configures it.

A useful analogy might be the contrast between a caravan leader and an automobile driver. Centuries ago, before there were roads of any significant character, most distant, overland travel went by caravan. Because solo travellers would most likely succumb to marauders, bandits, accidents, or disease, even if they did not get lost, it was necessary for people to group together in one large convoy that would be headed by someone who knew the territory, and had the vital expertise, not to mention the arms to defend his troupe from attacks. As roads improved, together with facilities along the way, the possibilities of travel on one's own became less risky. Nowadays the driver of a 'horseless carriage' can easily make it from Point A to Point B without anything resembling a 'caravan'. If the car breaks down, all he or she has to do is wait for a policeman to arrive, or to pick up a mobile phone and call for assistance.

Travelling the information superhighway

When there was no 'information superhighway', most intellectual travel required 'caravans' – residential classrooms – and 'caravan leaders' – teachers at the head of the class on a daily basis. But the 'highway' of today appears increasingly more like the federal road system of the 1950s than the muddy tracks through the wilderness that met, for example, Marco Polo in the thirteenth century. When bandwidth increases and copyright issues are finally sorted out in the next ten years, the new 'I-way' will probably resemble the inter-state system of the present day.

Imagine a Medieval guild of caravan leaders coming to President Eisenhower in 1956, when construction of the interstate system first got underway, and telling him that they still were responsible for all traffic from New York to Los Angeles, or Miami to Seattle. The scenario sounds absurd, but that perspective in fact is not too remote from what 'traditionalists' in the learning establishing are actually saying. The internet, in fact, is the information super-highway, and it is offering all the necessary provisions for the mind to transit in an infinity of directions. Driving the information superhighway still requires 'support personnel' – technology trainers, research specialists, information analysts, etc. – in the same way that cruising the interstate system depends on the avail-ability of gas stations, mechanics, state troopers, motels, conveni-ence stores, and fast-food restaurants. But the caravan leader is of lesser importance.

The analogy, of course, is incomplete, because concentrated and long-cultivated expertise in the knowledge business is more signifi-cant than simply being out front in a cortege. The age of information will always need knowledge specialists, and even subject specialists to contend with difficult and complex issues, not to mention pushing back the frontiers of science and learning itself. Ironically, when the trend over the past twenty years in higher education in particular has been toward de-emphasizing research by faculty and pushing them more toward classroom teaching, the digital revolution is confining the importance of face-to-face instruction to advanced problem solving and driving the role of teaching back dramatically in the direction of research.

Blurring the lines between teaching and research

As it turns out, the relationship between 'teaching' and 'research' in the digital era becomes increasingly blurry. The two terms, which presuppose the older model of knowledge, connote a world in which knowledge is conveyed, rather than constantly engendered from its own rootstock. A better phrase for these professional processes within the third knowledge revolution might be collaborative inquiry. The word 'inquiry' implies the acquisition of new understanding by an act of scrutiny, or by presenting questions. While the terms 'teaching' and 'learning' designate a strict division of labour that is inherently unequal, the notion of collaborative inquiry levels the playing field to a certain degree and lays the responsibility for 'discovery' on everyone involved in the knowledge enterprise. As in the world of commerce and politics, the new paradigm does not focus so much on whether individuals 'succeed' or 'fail', but whether innovation advances, and whether there are significant, socially useful or economically beneficial results.

This arrangement for years has been fairly common in the sciences, particularly in graduate research programmes and in laboratories. But the coming of the internet means the pragmatic, research prototype can now be extended across the span of education, and backwards to earlier ages in the process of schooling. Young children can be just as 'inquiring' as Ph.D. physicists. In the past they have not been able to 'collaborate' with either their peers or their elders on projects because access to curricular resources was far more restricted.

The bent of computer-mediated instruction (perhaps 'computer-mediated inquiry' is the *bon mot*) toward active learning and collaborative investigation is prompted, however, by far more important factors than the profusion of information on the internet. The bias is in the nature of the person/machine interface itself. Before the explosion of internet usage just a few years ago, the relationship of the human mind to the personal computer could be described primarily in more familiar terms of master and servant. Despite all the mythology dating back to an earlier era about computers dominating human beings, the PC revolution in the 1980s created a powerful and progressively user-friendly work tool for people engaged in conventional tasks. While there was much philosophical speculation about the future of computer-based 'artificial intelligence' the computer was becoming a sophisticated drone for such routine activities as computation, data management, and word processing. It had not yet made a difference with respect to the very essence of social and intellectual experience.

The internet, on the other hand, has generated that difference almost overnight. The deciding factor has been the way in which information can be rapidly shipped back and forth over an infinitely complex network between client and server, and between server and server. In an interesting fashion the architecture of information transport on the internet bears some comparison with the neural structure of the brain itself. In the brain, neural pathways are constantly being forged and electrical impulses routed, and rerouted, in the most efficient manner. Interestingly, the Department of Defence's design of the internet as a hubless network with limitless routing options through the so-called 'TCP/IP' system of protocols created the kind of vast, 'system intelligence' that the internet has actually become in its mode of operation.

This unbounded system intelligence creates a kind of 'mind' of its own. It is no longer a machine, but what we might call a 'meta-machine'. It is intelligence fostered through computer networks that are defined not by topography, but by the non-spatial method of 'addressing' – the so-called 'internet protocol'. When we add the human subject engaged in the act of exploration we have indeed the rudiments of a whole new standard of intelligence. The complex relationship between the student, the PC, and the network add up to a trivalent type of interface that gives rise to a different kind of intellectual universe than we have ever encountered. Furthermore, the internet itself is the ensemble of these myriad, trivalent complexes. The total 'intelligence' in the system is immense. Like all intelligent systems, there is a kind of 'cumulative' learning that takes place over time. We will give a few simple illustrations here to show what exactly we have in mind.

By 'intelligence' we mean something quite straightforward – an inherent ability of a system, which can of course include the human brain, to learn. Say I am a basic learner, and I want to find something on the 'net' concerning the history of Rome to complete a school assignment. If I am in a traditional class, I have probably been given an essay question or a 'paper topic', which I then dutifully research, write up, and hand back to the teacher. I may not even have to use a personal computer. I can do the research through the simple point-and-click methodology of a Web-TV. In effect, I have simply used the internet as an electronic reference tool. There is very little qualitative difference between this educational approach and the one that has persisted for centuries. And the only 'intelligence' that resides in this system is what is located in the grey matter beneath my skull. But suppose I am using a personal computer to access the internet, and the teacher gives me the assignment in the following format: Explain to the best of your ability why Rome fell, then post your answer on a newsgroup for critical response from your classmates.

To do the assignment I use a search engine by keying in the proper terms: 'Rome' and 'fall'. In contrast with a conventional library search, the medium of the internet gives me a larger permutation of related themes, inasmuch as I am not dependent on book or magazine titles *per se* to define the options I have in front of me. Depending on how thorough or diligent I am in pursuing my subject, which may involve consulting a variety of books as well, I have completed a fairly standard, and not necessarily exemplary, assignment. But let us imagine that I post my answer to a newsgroup. I get feedback. I receive other critical comments. I become part of a collaborative process that in the past was rare even in the most airy and refined heights of academia. My assignment is emailed around the net. My theory of why Rome fell is passed to professional scholars, some of whom give me more feedback via email and incorporate my ideas into their own writings. New thinking about the fall of Rome no longer is contingent, as in the old pattern of scholarship, on the publication of an occasional provocative thesis that attains some popular notoriety. The public nature of what I say or do is instantaneous. And its 'publication' is augmented by the regular, relentless, and many-faceted streams of input that it receives from all over the internet. Because communication on the internet is a constant, free-flowing 'conversation', both learning and intelligence are always marching forward.

Traditionalists, of course, argue that the lack of rigour and polish in what comes across the net is a sure sign that networked learning undermines 'standards'. But what they really mean is that they will not have the power as gatekeepers to allow what goes into the mind of the learner, and to censure what they want to keep out. The fact that the personal computer with its 'TCP/IP stack' of software has now become a communications device also contributes to this new picture. As an inquiring mind, I can process whatever information I encounter on the internet through the programs that are resident on my machine. There are a variety of ways I perform these tasks, and the 'orchestration' of information that I pull from the net involves a combination of familiar programs from word and image processing to 'FTP'. In fact, learning to toggle back and forth between the different kinds of internet sites and the programs that run on the PC is a kind of educational 'art form', resembling piano-playing. The counterpoints, harmonies, and intricate rhythms of cognition that can be produced are impressive indeed. Client-centred learning, once mastered, can be a powerful tool for the accrual of what we know in the way that knowledge in the contemporary era is unremittingly on the rise. Client-centred learning is not so much about the command of established, educational 'content' as about the capacity to birth new content. The collaborative nature of such learning makes this trend in education inevitable.

Expanding the conception of knowledge

The educational experience that emerges from the immersion of the mind in digital, or so-called 'virtual', reality is far different, yet at the same time inconceivably richer, than what the old 'institutional' structures have provided in the past. In the long run what has been learned in 'school' throughout most of the twentieth century will be viewed by cultural historians in the same way that the abacus is viewed by people today who employ spreadsheets and electronic calculators. The three 'R's' will still be venerated as the foundation of knowledge, but the means of expanding that knowledge have been amazingly expanded, if not superseded. The time-honoured idea of the 'student' will pass on into the notion of the 'learner', which in turn will be absorbed into the concept of the 'inquirer'. The functional differentiation between those who teach and those who are taught will give place to a new, integral vision of those who conspire for truth and understanding. The internet is not just another resource for learning. It is fast becoming the incubator of knowledge.

The third knowledge revolution is swiftly spilling over into a learning revolution. Over time the result of this revolution will be that the hallowed ivy halls will end up as a desolate ruin in the field, like some Medieval stone castle overlooking the Rhine. But before we analyse these new structures further, we need to understand the new, philosophical world view upon which it is grounded.

Chapter 4

The internet protocol and the emergence of a digital learning architecture

> I used to think that cyberspace was fifty years away. What I thought was fifty years away, was only ten years away. And what I thought was ten years away . . . it was already here. I just wasn't aware of it yet.
>
> (Bruce Sterling)

The third knowledge revolution is characterized by one of the most startling developments in the history of culture – the ascendancy of the 'internetwork'. In the educational arena this development translates straightaway into the idea that learning is not something that 'happens' to, or befalls, a particular learner, but a vast and complex enterprise that resonates in different ways from mind to mind, from junction to junction, or from site to site.

The fundamental metaphor for the third knowledge revolution, of course, is the 'internetwork'. The expression 'internet' is just a shorthand term for this network of networks. Some of the most basic principles and concepts of the science of networking are useful to entertain here before exploring the ways in which this development affects knowledge itself.

All networks have a distinct architecture, consisting of nodes, points and channels. A node is defined in the engineering literature as any device that is hooked up somehow to a network. A node is where an operator is able to make use of the network, or to use it in some important way to gain or manipulate information. A point simply describes a piece of spatial topography where there is some change in the network. A channel is a trajectory by which two or more nodes are able to communicate, or share information. In the lingo of the computer industry channels are now more familiar to us as 'links' or 'paths'.

From the standpoint of cognitive science, a node is that portion of a network that exhibits 'intelligence'. It is where significant modes of information input and output are possible, and where intelligent transformations of the data or content in the network can take place. The emergence of the internet over the past two decades has been earmarked by an evolution in the intelligence of the 'node', which in turn has allowed for an incredible expansion of the capacity of the network both to carry different kinds of traffic and to generate an elaborate system of interlinkages – hence the phrase 'internet'.

When the internet began as a proprietary network for stitching together computers within the Department of Defence, its distinctive asset was its 'connectivity'. In other words, it was designed to make sure that any computing device could find channels for communicating with any other computing device at any time. The strategy was to make the network invulnerable to nuclear attack or sabotage. In the early days of the internet, when the system passed on from the defence department to colleges and universities, the internet was still noted for its connectivity more than its intelligence. The architecture of the network was heavy with mainframe, and the preponderance of nodes were not PCs, but 'dumb terminals'.

The invention of a 'client' software known as 'Winsock' that would run on Windows – by now the exclusive operating system for the PC – was responsible largely for the changeover. Coupled with the first graphics-intensive web browsers, such as Mosaic and the first edition of Netscape, Winsock software made it possible for the system intelligence to shift over from mainframes to personal computers. Such applications as client email, internet relay chat, audio streaming and TCP/IP video conferencing offered a means by which the original vision of an 'information superhighway' over which anything that could be called digital might travel and be piped right to the client. The idea of the 'highway', first enunciated by government officials in the early 1990s, of course did not envision the internet. It presupposed at first that most 'interactivity' would be limited to people making selections of entertainment, or products to purchase, on their television screens. It failed to take account of the manner in which the personal computer would 'push' information onto the networks rather than merely 'pulling' in pre-packaged and premium-priced content in accordance with the model of cable television.

The difference is intelligence

The difference between the internet and the old computer networks is comparable to the difference between the PC and the old 'dumb terminals'. The difference is one of intelligence. In short, the internet by its very nature is a 'smart network'. The creation of a network with constantly evolving, built-in intelligence can only revolutionize education and training because by its very makeup it is supplying enormous amounts of the 'intellectual' capital that economists frequently theorize about, but have a hard time identifying specifically.

The elaborate, or even labyrinthine, nature of the internet accounts for the creation of intelligence at the macro-level. However, the transport of information throughout such a complex mesh of conduits would not be possible without the so-called 'internet protocol' which contributes to the network's intelligence at the micro-level. In fact, it is the internet protocol which has made the growth of the net itself possible. Information over the internet does not travel directly from one location to another. Prior to the internet, most data travelled directly over 'circuits', which were connected to switches and then routed to their destinations. The historic telephone networks, including the ones we still use to call Aunt Sarah in Syracuse or Uncle Alfred in Albania, have been built on this kind of arrangement. Such networks operate on a 'point-to-point' protocol, and the entire economics of the telephone industry has been based on metering and charging for the amount of electrons that flow between points.

It is the same in the diminutive world of bytes and bits as it is with the air transportation system. If I want to fly directly between two of the major airline hubs, such as Chicago and Los Angeles, I usually have little problem finding a cheap or convenient flight. If, however, I want to fly from Chicago to Topeka, Kansas I will have to go directly to one city – perhaps Kansas City – and be 'switched' to a computer flight that will take me to my destination. The ticket for the commuter flight may cost as much as the cost of travelling from Chicago to Kansas City. The same is true if I want to make a call from Chicago to Kansas City. I can probably obtain a fairly decent rate. But calling, or flying, between Kansas City and Topeka costs me just about as much as making the same point-to-point transit from Chicago to Kansas City, if not more. The reason is economics. In a point-to-point architecture the frequency of traffic between two locations is significant from a cost standpoint. Hence, a point-to-point system is intrinsically vulnerable to disruption and changes in traffic patterns.

The internet protocol

The internet protocol was invented to get around these types of problems. Transmission of data over the internet does not proceed directly between points through circuits and switches. The internet employs something known as 'packet switching' which, even though it sounds similar, is quite different from what goes on in circuit switched networks. In the former environment messages are broken down at the source into 'packets' of data which are then conveyed by a variety of often circuitous routes to their goal. The packets are reassembled into the original message at their destination. Unlike point-to-point communication where the entirety of the message is transported over the same channel in keeping with the principle of the shortest distance between source and target, a packet-switched network relies on a multitude of possible pathways over which it can route fractions of a message with the aim of delivering them to their objective in the shortest time.

The concept of packet-switching is as old as the design of a courier service in times of warfare. When a messenger has to traverse dangerous territory to carry a dispatch from one command post to another, there is always a likelihood he will be killed or detained. There was also the very real possibility the message itself would be intercepted. To make sure the message got through, military leaders would often send the same message, even if it was coded, in different forms by different couriers.

But the use of carrier pigeons would be a better analogy. The homing instincts of carrier pigeons are trained in such a way that the bird will always wind up at the correct location, even if they wing away from their departure point in totally different directions. Let us presume we have a letter we want to send by carrier pigeon from Memphis to Pittsburgh. The normal method would be to strap a message to the leg of one of the birds and dispatch it along that route. That describes exactly point-to-point transmission. But what if we take the same piece of paper and tear it into small shreds, then lash each piece to a different pigeon? That describes the internet protocol. The different birds will find different ways of going to Pittsburgh, and they most likely will not even arrive at once. Once all the pigeons have arrived, we can paste all the different pieces of paper together and reconstruct the message that was initially transmitted.

The second technique simulates the internet protocol. In the case of the internet, the scraps of paper attached to pigeons are the 'packets'. The packets have their own electronic 'homing instinct'. It is known as the 'IP (internet protocol) address'. IP addresses are numbers separated by dots, such as '399.45.03.111'. These numbers are translated into 'addresses' such as 'www.thisbook.com'. The packet always 'knows' to go to the address that is coded into it, whether that address is five miles away or fifteen thousand miles away. The packets may whiz from node to node all over a global network, but they are ultimately directed to the IP address in question. The devices that read the address codes and send them toward their destination are known as routers. Routers are also used to join subnetworks that are similar in design.

The internet works the amazing way it does because it does not matter what kind of machines are hooked up to it, what kinds of operating systems they have, what kinds of 'local area networks' (LANs) or 'wide area networks' (WANs) comprise the subnetworks. The architecture of the internet is as potentially intricate and indefinable as the geography of the planet itself. However, there are critical zones where the architectures of large subnetworks do not mesh. A simple example would be the telephone lines over which a computer 'dialup' system operates and the internet itself. The devices that demarcate these two zones are known as gateways. Gateways 'translate' streams of data from one system to another and are the most crucial dimension of internet connectivity. Within the different subnetworks there are also junctions or 'fittings' that demand special hardware applications. A very important application is the *bridge*. The purpose of a bridge is to separate one segment of a network from another. Bridges are capable of interconnecting local area networks and to create what are known in the trade as 'internet backbones'. In addition to bridges, these subnetworks requires *hubs*. A hub serves as a switching centre. It centralizes the different circuits, or channels, over which the packets in the process of information exchange travel.

The picture that falls together, therefore, is one of co-ordination of voluminous information transport across a mazelike terrain of fibres, wires, and aerial transmitters. The notion of the internet is something far more significant and mind-arresting than the conventional view of the electronic network that has long been the stock-in-trade of the engineering profession. How does the elaboration of this 'internetwork' contribute to the knowledge revolution itself? We have already discussed the way in which internetworking sets off an explosion of system intelligence. Yet it has even more telling impact. Internetworking makes possible the constant reinterpretation of any given message that enters the system.

For example, an email or newsgroup correspondent may send off a thought or opinion in the form of a 'thread' – which indeed may be a response to a response to a response, and so on. When one 'posts' to a newsgroup, or to a mass mailing programme known as a 'listserve', the message is fair game for anybody to do anything with it they wish. They can forward it to other newsgroups or listserves. They can incorporate it into a web page. Or, most importantly, they can offer critical replies and re-directioning of the original message *ad infinitum*. This constant reintegration of a sequence of messages into new messages, or threads, is what most classical philosophers of education agreed was the key to understanding a body of knowledge. It is the *power of interpretation*. The technical term for the science of interpretation is 'hermeneutics', derived from the name of the Greek god Hermes who was the message-bearer. The internet makes possible the endless expansion of intelligence because it is fundamentally a self-propelled 'hermeneutical' system. For centuries the goal of humanistic education was to teach students how to interpret the material they have learned. The Bible, of course, was until this century the most valuable material anyone in school might master. And the Bible was never something merely to be received by the learner. It had to be interpreted in order to be intelligible. The wealth of Biblical interpretation, and the profusion over the millennia of both Jewish and Christian sects with divergent readings of what the Bible is supposed to mean, attests to the complexity of this process.

The unique way in which the internet functions as a hermeneutical system is suggested in the origin of the word 'internet' itself. The internet was invented and contrived to join an infinite number of computers with different operating systems by a single protocol. The explosive growth of the internet has been an immediate result of such an 'open' network architecture. In other words, the internet is not just a 'network of networks', as it has been commonly called, but in principle an ever enlarging and intricate galaxy of signals and connections. From a structural standpoint the only physical phenomenon, therefore, that can be compared to the internet is the human brain itself. With its unimaginable possibilities and permutations of neural assembly and operations, the human brain has the same kind of open biological 'architecture' as does the internet. While individual computers are limited with respect to the processing power of their central operating chips, the limitless connectivity of the internet introduces a factor that can only be understood in terms of the new science of cognitive psychology. In recent years cognitive psychology has made tremendous scientific strides in demonstrating the relationship between intelligent activity, or thought, and the biophysical character of information processing. Cognitive psychology has succeeded to a certain degree in striding the giant chasm in Western philosophy between the respective realities we term 'mind' and 'body'.

We do not want to carry the analogy too far between the 'intelligence' of the internet and that of the brain. But it is useful to note that the common factor of reticulated connectivity is what distinguishes both kinds of 'systems' from other kinds, natural as well as artificial. The complexity of these conjunctive links and electrical messaging increases at an exponential magnitude as new components of the system are added, and new modes of coherence are achieved.

Although we tend to think of the internet primarily as a marvellous medium of digital communication, the truth is that the element of intelligence and the 'weaving' of knowledge belongs to its very makeup. In fact, this weaving of countless strands, contact points, and interfaces explains why the metaphor of the 'world wide web' was concocted to capture the sense of the marvellous intricacy and internal correspondences of the graphic version of the internet. What is decisive about a 'web' is that it precedes all its authors and producers. The medium is not simply the message; it is also the method. That is, the world wide web serves as the set of conditions through which knowledge in the postmodern era is generated, and becomes possible in the first place. As Mark Taylor notes, a web 'is neither subjective nor objective and yet is the matrix in which all subjects and objects are formed, deformed, and reformed. In the postmodern culture of simulacra, we are gradually coming to realize that complex communication webs and information networks, which function holistically but not totalistically, are the milieu in which everything arises and passes away'.[27] The web is much more than a descriptive principle. It is an all-pervasive kind of facticity that arrives with the epoch of digital commerce and communications. Over time it becomes the arbiter of all artifacts of thought, culture and understanding.

As the internet continues to evolve and envelop the planet, the precept of 'webbed information' (which is the chrysallis of the new knowledge revolution itself) comes to dominate over segmented, or compartmentalized, realms of experience and discovery. The internet is not, and can never be, simply a means of passive enjoyment. Despite tireless efforts by the broadcast or retail industries to co-opt it, the internet withstands every attempt to make it some sort of counterpart to movies and television, or the suburban shopping mall. The internet is the learning medium par excellence, not some new entertainment bonanza, mainly because its workings bespeak something more akin to an active mind than to a passive form of data transmission. The internet does not attain this status simply as a labyrinth of copper or fibre wiring, software overlays, and crosstalk between pieces of computer hardware. It reaches that plateau because of the way in which its physical 'interoperability' allows for ever sophisticated means of integrating the native intelligence of the countless system 'operators'. The philosopher René Descartes inaugurated the whole of modern philosophy over three centuries ago with the simple assertion of mental reality 'I think, therefore I am'. A similar precept of the new cyberreality might be encapsulated in this phrase: 'I link, therefore, I am more than I was before'. That is also the key principle of learning in the digital age.

bollox

Implications of the digital learning architecture

The tremendous theoretical implications of the new digital learning architecture are only dimly understood, let alone comprehended. To get some sense of what is happening from a pure, conceptual standpoint, we need to explore the way in which the technological combination of digital signalling and network reticularity provides a real-world simulation of the 'dialectical' form of thought that has overshadowed nineteenth and twentieth-century philosophy. Though dialectical thinking is popularly associated with rarefied types of Germanic philosophy, its principles are fundamental to the Western intellectual, and therefore 'educational', tradition.

It was Socrates, of course, who in ancient Athens gave us not only the dialectical method of philosophy, but the basic theory of modern education with its stress on intellectual striving and inquiry. 'Dialectic', as the etymology of the Greek term suggests ('dia' = between, 'logos' = discourse), entails a constant clash of the binary elements of language. Digital 'logic', as we all know by now, is the proffering of advanced computational 'arguments' by means of infinite combinations of '1s' and '0's', or arrangements of 'yes' and 'no'. It was the genius of the nineteenth-century philosopher Georg Wilhelm Hegel to take Socrates' method of sequential 'yea-saying' and 'nay-saying' and develop it into what he called 'speculative thought', where everything stated or denied is constantly trans-formed into new and higher-order statements and denials.

In the Hegelian universe that which 'is' instantly passes over into that which 'is not', and that which 'is not' negates itself to become something that 'is' again, but in a more developed or substantive sense. Hegelian thinking is comparable, though not perfectly comparable, to digital thinking.

Hegel recognized early in his distinguished career that the system of 'dialectic' must somehow be embodied in a concrete setting to be effective. In other words, Hegelian 'logic' is ultimately not meta-physical, but historical. Hegel's insistence that history itself is dialec-tical became the basis of so much political thinking in the Western world from the time of the French Revolution onwards. 'The real is rational, and the rational is real' was one of his more famous utter-ances.[28] Hegel called human history the 'march of the world spirit', and the march is dialectical. Likewise, the dialectical nature of com-puter intelligence takes on its own kind of 'world historical' (to use Hegel's idiom) aspects in the emergence of so-called 'internetworks'. The dialectical principle runs throughout the whole of human society, and demolishes ancient or perduring structures wherever it comes across them. 'Creative destruction' reigns!

This notion of 'creative destruction', which the economist Joseph Schumpeter first applied to the institutions of capitalism early in the twentieth century, is even more pertinent to internet connectivity, and thereby to the movement of knowledge itself. The stagger-ing pace at which innovations in the current digital technology are occurring cannot be explained solely as an accident of history. As planetary civilization becomes 'digitized', every cultural and symbolic form, including the basic configurations of language and self-understanding, are rapidly and constantly tossed into turmoil. Every instant of intelligence is in principle ready to be interlaced with every other instant of intelligence, begetting the kind of system intelligence we have already described. It would be foolish to indulge in the kind of pseudo-religious abstractions to which Hegel himself succumbed, postulating that the internet is some kind of overarching, or abstract 'divinity' transcending human consciousness. But in a certain sense the internet has, and will more obviously in the future take on, a life of its very own.

The metaphor of an evolving, collective intelligence as it denotes the internet, therefore, makes more sense than the more familiar manner of typifying it as a 'virtual community'. Communitarian sentiments were prominent in the shaping of the original ideology of the internet before it became the digital medium of choice for the millennium. But these sentiments have less to do with the technology itself than with the Sixties-bred utopianism of the early pioneers on the 'electronic frontier'. The ideal of the virtual community grew because the internet in its early phase was for the most part a tightly bound crew of techies and new communications specialists who had discovered a way to keep in touch and share their lives in a distinctive manner. Inasmuch as the internet constituted a method by which people with common desires and interests could instantly overcome the limitations of space and the high communications costs historically associated with enormous distance, the romance of the global, online community quickly came into play.

To a certain extent the countless subcultures and subject niches centred around chatrooms and newsgroups continue to stoke such idyllic interpretations of what is really happening. But evidence from social psychology is starting to accumulate that the internet does not necessarily make individuals more social, or enable them to engage more fruitfully in what we normally understand as social interaction. On the contrary, the anonymity of the internet often brings out unconscious, anti-social tendencies that might otherwise be suppressed in face-to-face engagement. In addition, such much-publicized 'disorders' at internet addiction and compulsive surfing lend credence to the assertion that 'virtual community' often can become a kind of theatre of individual instincts and wishes that allows more for psychodrama and acting out scripts of personal alienation than joining people together joyously and responsibly.

In truth, the internet at a primitive level functions more like what the twentieth-century philosophical psychologist Carl Jung termed the 'collective unconscious' than the rational and conscious institutions of human society – that dark, barely articulate dynamism of human experience that affects and motivates individuals as well as entire peoples through dream, myth, art and fantasy. It is not so much a social force as a neuro-electrical, but non-biological catalyst for new levels of human cognition. In the same way that emotional and imaginative experience is a necessary precursor to intellectual development, so the kind of massive information synthesis that takes place in online computing promotes higher levels of social intelligence. The relationship between internet use and social intelligence defines, furthermore, its importance to what we have in the past called 'education'.

Indeed, the original inventors of the graphics form of the internet are now pursuing what they call 'the semantic web', which will come close to simulating, if not surpassing, advanced human intelligence. Using the 'extensible markup language', or XML, it will rely on mapping the complexities of human literary communication with its grammar, shadowings, and syntax, rather than strictly on the binary number crunching that distinguishes most of today's computer operations. The semantic web will also make use of two additional layers of digital cognitive aids – the 'resource description framework' (RDF), which serves both as a word-definition pool and a thesaurus, and an 'ontology', which figures out the intricate relationships between the markup language and the conceptual matrix. For example, following the sense of context on which the most basic forms of interpretative skills depend, the 'intelligent agents' of the semantic web will be able to tell easily the difference between a ZIP code and a phone number, which currently is not possible with internet search engines. Timothy Berners-Lee, designer of the world wide web and now the commandante in the development of the semantic web, anticipates that this second-generation approach to internetworking will bring about 'a new age of enlightenment'. It will 'help more people become more intuitive as well as more analytical. It will foster global collaborations among people with diverse cultural perspectives, so we have a better chance of finding the right solutions to the really big issues'.[29] The semantic web will succeed in sorting and integrating information according to semantic rules or decision-trees that digital intelligence heretofore has not even approximated.

As Dewey impressed on us so well, social intelligence is the ultimate aim of all public activities, and education for that reason is the most vital of public institutions. The internet is fast becoming the great reservoir of unformulated social experience. It is the job of educators to convert that experience into social intelligence.

possible reading

Beyond education

for cybercultural
perspehves

The age of transaction and the 'scene' of digital learning

> The dogmas of the quiet past are inadequate for the stormy present and future. As our circumstances are new, we must think anew, and act anew.
>
> (Abraham Lincoln)

The current knowledge revolution renders obsolete what less than a decade ago was called 'educational reform'. The crux of educational reform has always consisted in retooling the instructional institutions of a society to meet new goals, satisfy collective desires and expectations, or mobilize economic and intellectual resources in a different strategic fashion.

Waves of educational reform usually accompany periods of wholesale social change. The development of 'progressive education' earlier this century was a response to rapid industrialization and urbanization. The preoccupation with science and mathematics in the late 1950s and early 1960s grew out of national anxiety about the expanding military power and global political influence of the Soviet Union. The move to define standards for subject and skills mastery and to create a 'core curriculum' during the late 1980s was an immediate reaction to the social flux and cultural upheavals of the previous decades that had led to a loss of purpose for public education, or what had once been called 'the common school'.

The changes now underway, however, are of a sizably different order. Whereas the education reform movements of the past did not alter the basic social infrastructure in which knowledge was created, the current revolution involves a transmutation in the way in which the world is experienced in its entirety. An interesting example is Finn and Rebarber's *Education Reform in the 90s* published in 1992. Cited by many academic reformers less than a half-decade ago as a graphic roadmap of the issues and tasks supposedly lying immediately ahead, the book touches on everything that just a few short years later is entirely uninteresting or irrelevant. It mentions school choice and restructuring, designing accountability models, overcoming the acceptance of mediocrity. The authors opine at the outset: 'only when we all understand the direction in which we are traveling do we have a prayer of getting where we want to be'.[30] Ironically, there is virtually no mention of digital technology. The gales are blowing. The waves are billowing. The direction of the ship has shifted dramatically.

The end of 'teaching'

During the last reform cycle social consensus seemed to support the notion that teaching was the *summum bonum*, the 'highest good', in the educational universe. In one sense the exaltation of this value was an upshot of the cultural upheavals of the Sixties. The student riots in Berkeley during the early portion of that decade were in protest to the impersonal character of higher education. A consensus that the business of the professoriate was not to engage almost exclusively in private research, no matter the social and economic benefits, but to roll up its sleeves, spend far more hours in the classroom, and do something took on a mystical connotation of its own. Books and articles describing the subtle and salubrious art of teaching piled up. Politicians passed legislation designed to reward teaching and discourage what was perceived as a self-gratifying and excessive professionalism on the part of the educracy. The 'master teacher', whoever that might be, became a minor cultural icon.

Interestingly, the push to reinstate the role of teaching was never matched by an equally fervent curiosity about the quality and tenor of learning. The covert assumption was that good teaching automatically begets learning. The assumption was always a sort of Protestant presumption, i.e. *sound preaching inculcates righteousness*. In effect, the preoccupation with the promotion of teaching during the reform period may constitute the last hurrah of the 'Protestant principle' in education. As George Marsden has observed, the history of American education in general, and higher education in particular, has been a struggle between the yearning for spiritual advancement and the relentless pressures of a technological economy.[31] In one sense the advent of digital learning means the latter force has triumphed, but in another way it also points toward the realization of the value of individual freedom in an institutional matrix – a supreme value in its own right.

As the trend toward digital instruction gathers force, a kind of new 'Copernican revolution' can be discerned. Just as Copernicus redefined astronomy by positing that the earth circles around the sun, and not the other way around, so the new educational theory suggests that the generation of knowledge must be pegged to the conditions of the learner, rather than the genius of the instructor. As Sir John Daniel, chancellor of the British Open University, professed so eloquently during a keynote speech at the 1998 *Syllabus* conference in Sonoma, California, the revolution is about 'learning', not 'teaching'.

Daniel's dictum will most likely cause untold consternation among generations of educational reformers who have learned to intone the seemingly self-legitimating mantra that the business of education is teaching, and that the reward and encouragement of good teaching will somehow yield a more knowledgeable and learned society. One of the difficulties with this well-nigh sacred doctrine is that no one has ever come near to agreement on what signifies good teaching. That is not to say the debate is specious, or that teaching is not an art form that needs to be praised and celebrated into the next millennium. But the advent of digital culture poses a set of issues that the classical debates over knowledge and education have never factored together satisfactorily.

Before proceeding further on this thread, we need to attain some clarity concerning what the terms 'teaching' and 'learning' mean with respect to the philosophy of education. As it turns out, these words are somewhat loaded, and carry with them varying connotations, and are to a certain degree, though not exclusively, culture-bound. The history of civilization harbours various archetypes of teaching and learning, as well as assumptions about how the two functions link to each other. We can distinguish five general and operative archetypes that still affect us today.

Historical archetypes of teaching and learning

The first archetype of teaching and learning is what I will call the *mandarin*. The mandarin model harks back to the imperial courts of China, though it has been implemented in various forms throughout Western civilization, particularly in the royal dynasties of the ancient Near East. In the mandarin view the principal purpose of teaching is *transmission* of ancient cultural norms, practices, and values. Rote instruction, including extensive memorization and mastery of select skills such as reading and calligraphy, dominates over the use of any kind of critical intelligence or inquiry. Mandarin instruction has historically gone hand-in-hand with political abso-lutism and despotism. Learning is essentially a replication of tasks and information that are considered socially and ideologically acceptable. Deviations from these restrictive procedures are either discouraged or severely repressed in order to guarantee over time a complex of social protocols, thoughts, or habits of behaviour.

The second is the *academic*. By 'academic' we do not have in mind the broader use of the term in the popular lexicon. We are referring to the technical denotation of the word as it derives from the ancient Greek academy in Athens. The academic archetype is the corner-stone of the modern idea of a 'liberal arts' education. It focuses on the self-development of the learner by means of a challenging and charismatic role model in the person of the teacher. In the academic model the role of teaching is to produce, as the cliché goes today, 'lifelong learners'. In most respects it is the converse of the mandarin, in the same way the Athenian democracy that spawned it is the historical antithesis of the great Oriental empires with whom it often contended. The academic archetype revolves around the ideal of critical thinking, and is enshrined in the legend of Socrates who claimed to know nothing and taught both his students and his adversaries to examine ruthlessly their presuppositions and opinions. Despite aspirations, especially during the last decade, to make the academic archetype a benchmark for educational reform in the Western democracies, the truth is that so-called 'liberal learn-ing' has always been, and will remain, a luxury for social elites in a democratic culture. Just as the 'academics' of ancient Athens were always members of the privileged strata of society, so they are today, even when they mouth egalitarian slogans and visions.

The third archetype we shall call the *clerical*. The clerical arche-type is quintessentially Western, which encompasses the world of Islam, and reflects the historical role of religious hierarchies in shaping secular institutions from the Caucasus to the British Isles. According to the clerical archetype, the goal of instruction is to inculcate in the student the kinds of beliefs, values, and moral prac-tices that will demonstrate that they are, first, worthy of eternal

salvation and, second, capable of living a virtuous and socially productive life. In conventional discourse we would call this process
'character building'. The function of learning is self-development,
as in the academic model. But self-development does not mean
open-ended expansion of individual potentialities, as in the case of
liberal learning. Instead learning signifies the growth of one's understanding of, and commitment to, their role as one of God's creatures.
Practical knowledge and skills are important in the clerical archetype, but they always remain subordinate to concerns about one's
eternal destiny. In some respects the American liberal arts curriculum, particularly in parochial or sectarian schools, still flaunts clerical objectives. Yet the clerical model as a pure, if not dominant, form
of education has for the most part vanished in the contemporary era.

The fourth is the *industrial* archetype. Until recently the industrial
archetype was the prevalent type of educational arrangement in the
West as a whole, and in the United States specifically. The industrial
archetype is the organizational touchstone for most of American
education, including K-12 schooling, community college systems,
and the so-called 'comprehensive' or 'land grant university'. The
industrial model was first developed in the late nineteenth century
in imperial Germany and was imported immediately into the
United States by homegrown educational reformers. The industrial
archetype emerged as advocates of a strong nation-state and a capitalist economy discovered that workers at all levels must be increasingly equipped with scientific and technical know-how in order to
sustain social innovation and economic expansion. In an important
sense the industrial archetype consist in an adaptation of the clerical
archetype, except that the ideal of sophisticated skills training
replaced that of moral development. The corporation supplants
the church. Teaching remains a type of inculcation, and learning is
what today we would call 'competency-based'. The push for 'digital'
or computer-based instruction at present through so-called 'distance
learning' modalities has simply reproduced the industrial archetype.

To date much distance education is still a glorified variant of
corporate training, and the enthusiasm by which executives of
major technology firms have embraced digital learning testifies to
this trend. Paradoxically, however, the very principles of digital
learning militate against its co-optation by the new industrialists.
Because digital learning is client-centred and learner-driven, it can
never really become an instrument of corporate regimentation.
Political and educational conservatives who dream of harnessing

the social and economic power of networked personal computers to mould the educational system according to their proprietary and somewhat parochial interests are in for a rude awakening.

The fifth archetype, therefore, is something different from the industrial archetype. It is what we shall call the *transactional* archetype. One might expect that we would use terminology that was native somehow to the language of digital culture – e.g. 'informational' or 'cyber-' archetype, but these terms bespeak more the appearance rather than the substance of what is actually taking place at the level of education with the third knowledge revolution.

The transactional archetype

In the abstract the transactional archetype of teaching and learning could have evolved without the invention of the personal computer, and it may become the dominant regime of education when the PC with its keyboards, operating system, software, and network connectivity is a relic of the past. For example, the industrial system itself was originally propelled by the arrival of the steam engine, but later discarded the energy of vaporization as its material basis. Likewise, PCs may one day becoming nothing more than electric, or even optical, units of intelligence in every device that intrudes into our lives. Digital intelligence may be superseded in the same way that the firing of coal furnaces gave way to the combustion of petroleum distillates and eventually electricity. Yet the notion of transactional learning will persist, until another major historical transformation looms on the horizon.

In the transactional archetype teaching and learning are no longer separate activities, or even abilities, in the generation of knowledge. The universe of transactional learning is no longer bi-directional, but multi-polar with the numerous ripples and eddies of intellectual experience roiling about that centre of investigative activity we call the 'learner'.

In this regard Daniel's dictum is incomplete, because it lodges to a certain degree the fallacy of the new 'digital industrialists' who believe that learning will somehow take place by itself once there is enough technology, and an understanding of how to utilize the technology, on the part of the student, or 'client', population. The digital industrialists have a kind of sci-fi, or Star Trekian, picture in their heads of inherently smart systems of technology that are ubiquitous and provide automatic guidance for fallible denizens of cyberspace. The myth of the teacher as 'Hal the computer' dies hard. Unlike the industrial archetype which presumes that people are still passive learners taught not by clerics or corporate personnel, but by super-competent machines, the transactional archetype rides on what most analysts of the new digital technology take to be the distinguishing trait of cyberexperience itself – the opening of a universe of endless interactivity, or more precisely, 'transactivity'.

The concept of transactivity is crucial to grasping the educational experience wrought by digital culture. This experience transcends any particular kind of social, economic, or educational institution that may make a claim on that culture. In fact, it delimits a new 'learning space' itself. Because this new learning space transcends the bi-polar relationship between teaching and learning, it abolishes all former educational archetypes that have dominated in the past. In perhaps more than a simple metaphorical sense, it signifies the 'end of education' as the word has been used historically.

Recently the word 'learning space' has begun to circulate throughout the discourse concerning the new computer-mediated education. By learning space we mean the total context, or set of conditions, within which learning at a particular juncture takes place. The phrase 'any time, any place', which has become a kind of watchword for distance learning modalities as they have been configured for the internet, is an example of a basic kind of learning space. Heretofore the learning space of a typical class could be characterized by a teacher in front of a group of students, who listened, took notes, and asked questions. In a 'distributed learning' environment the learning space is considerably different. It can be classified as a complex and constantly shifting set of queries and responses on the part of both instructor and student. This perpetual give-and-take between teacher and learner renders the distinction between 'educator' and the 'educated' less significant. The word we propose is 'transactivity'.

Transactive learning upends the very distinction between teaching and learning as it has lodged in our understanding. In the past teaching and learning were viewed as specific, but separate, activities. Each activity, in turn, could be understood as having been performed by a singular 'agent'. By and large the former was regarded as active, the latter as passive. Education was perceived as an effort to 'produce' or 'bring forth' a result in someone. The etymology of the term 'education' (*educare* = to 'lead out of') reinforces this kind of analysis. Transactivity, on the other hand, means that the functions of 'teaching' and 'learning' take place simultaneously in both agents, formerly designated as instructors or students.

Transactive learning is the term most appropriate to the learning space of a digital culture with the contours of a 'world wide web'. It points not to the emergence of a new learning 'infrastructure' but to what John Gehl calls its 'metastructure' – a rethinking of the complete 'why' and 'wherefore' of learning.[32] The very idea of a global reticulation of intelligent machines and their operators engaged in an infinite process of exchanging information and creating 'sites' for commerce in that information necessitates this way of conceiving what we used to term 'educational activity'. Transactivity differs in a precise manner from what in the jargon we call 'inter-activity' – a goal toward which every educator, regardless of whether they are technologically savvy, strives. Whereas interactivity can be a localized event in what is otherwise an authoritarian or highly structured and traditional learning space, transactivity involves the whole of the learning space, and the 'learning culture' for that matter. For this reason the time period we have now entered may be dubbed 'the age of transaction'.

Broadly speaking, we can see that the learning spaces that have dominated in each of the historical archetypes we mentioned so far have reflected a conventional learning culture centred on *control of the classroom by the instructor*. Even the Socratic model with its stress on self-discovery and non-directive inquiry requires a kind of 'sage on the stage', or a 'star in the seminar'. At the most fundamental level all teaching and learning archetypes preceding the age of transaction were 'authorial', insofar as they were focused on the instructor both as the 'authority' within a particular discipline and as the originator of all academic content within the learning space. These authorial structures dominate both the popular and the professional mindset when we think of a general universe of learning that we call 'education'.

It would be foolish, if not unduly utopian, to postulate that in the era of transactive learning authorities, or some kind of authorial means of mediating knowledge to the student, are eliminated. The idea of the 'teacherless classroom', which some budget-gutting politicians dream about in their more derelict reveries, is a pure, and perilous, fantasy. As Athansios Moulakis has sardonically quipped, 'there is no teacher-proof method of teaching'.[33] However, that does not mean the pre-eminence of authorial instruction will go unchallenged. Quite the opposite! The proliferation of transactive learning spaces in the age of computer-mediated education signifies that control of the content of curriculum must give place to an explosion of self-crafted, *ad hoc*, and customized learning modules, where the great historical divide between instructor and student can be found in a state of meltdown. For more than one generation now developmental psychologists have been telling us that the play of children is an imaginative simulation of sophisticated learning initiatives. Transactive learning is not 'play' in the conventional sense of the word, but it exhibits the freedom and self-tutoring through immediate feedback that juvenile behaviour embodies.

Digital culture by its very character involves constant experimentation and exploratory activity. The infinite web of files and hyperlinks that constitute the 'internet' activates this movement of exploration. We are witnessing what one analyst of media culture terms a 'archetypeatic shift from linear text to overall pattern . . . fretted with radical epistemological, pedagogical, political, and organizational consequences'.[34] One of the criticisms offered by traditional pedagogy of web-based learning is that it does not allow sufficient content filtration and selection to be useful as an educational experience. But this view, which itself derives from the authorial standpoint, represents a failure to apprehend the means by which so-called 'web surfing', unless it is entirely random, has built-in mechanisms of selection. The hierarchy of 'hits' provided by the main search engines is a good example. Bad material increasingly finds its way to the electronic trash bin. With proper, general guidelines for content discrimination web voyagers can distinguish between the real and the bogus, the profound and the fatuous, more easily than any kind of magisterial privilege can facilitate.[35]

In short, the critical competencies honed in the *self-selection* of content are as vital to the outcome of so-called 'hyperlearning' with its unlimited transactivity as the highly prized skills of inquiry, judgement, and reflection are in the classic liberal arts setting. Whereas traditional book-based curriculum was by its very nature passive and therefore required authorial intervention, the new spaces of digital scholarship are wide-open and undulating spaces. Digital scholarship is truly the 'final frontier' of knowledge for this very reason.

Digital scholarship and the new scene of knowledge

Indeed, the notion of digital scholarship may be moving us in the very direction of the true 'open university' which educational visionaries have been touting, but failing to realize beyond the realms of rhetoric, for more than a generation. The picture is sketched by Robert and Jon Solomon in their irreverent book with a flavour of Sixties-style polemics entitled *Up the University.*

> The idea is to break down the barriers between faculty as well as between faculty and students and faculty and administrators. We are all in this educational mission together, and no one should be confined to an isolated role. We have a lot to learn from each other, teachers from students and administrators from teachers. What could give an administrator more of a sense of place in the university than actually to participate in its mission rather than 'watch over' its workings from above?[36]

Again, the vision is etheric and somewhat Arcadian. But the joke on educational radicals is that the new digital technology may make possible the kinds of academic democratization that were not historically convenient, or economically viable, in the past. A current, fashionable term which signifies this new set of circumstances is 'situated learning'. Situated learning means that the pedagogical process responds to signals generated by the intellectual environment itself. Learning is depicted as 'an integral part of generative practice in the lived-in world' instead of 'an isolated thing we do in schools'.[37] When Lenin was asked what enabled the Russian Revolution, his reply was simple: 'soviets plus electrification'. The Marxist analogy should not be pursued for obvious cause. But it is fair to note that the long-standing call to make the educational experience more team-driven and task-oriented could not have emerged without the powerful momentum of the new educational technology. Our answer to how we can reform the university, henceforth, may be disarmingly straightforward: 'collaborative groups plus digitization'.

Some significant empirical research carried out in the United Kingdom confirms that a collaborative learning infrastructure for computer-mediated instruction boosts standard educational outcomes.[38] But it would be a fallacy to presuppose that the expansion of online learning applications simply instantiates an already existing, and respectable, kind of progressive pedagogy. On the contrary, digital education points not only beyond education, but beyond pedagogy itself. The dynamism of an enveloping transactive, digital society ensures that, in the words of the French postmodernist philosopher Jean Baudrillard, that 'the real scene has been lost' and that we carry out our parts in a 'scene where you had rules for the game and some solid stakes that everybody could rely on'.[39]

Instead of familiar, but ultimately inconsequential talk about 'reforming education', 'transforming the classroom', or 'digitizing' the profession of teaching, perhaps we would be better served with language that connotes redescribing the 'scene' of knowledge. The word 'scene' is useful here because it carries the force of both a social locale of recurrent action and a moment in history itself. The French phrase *mise en scène* furnishes some of those connotations. If transactivity defines a special learning space for what we have conventionally called 'instruction', then it also identifies what we may dub the new millennial *scene of knowledge*. The knowledge revolution we are undergoing contextualizes all learning, and learning institutions, within that scene. It is a scene where the walls of the stage of invisible and the boundary between performance and audience is technically erased. It is a scene where many who are watching leap on the stage, on those who have been strutting before the footlights suddenly find themselves part of the onlookers. The scene is increasingly bi-directional. In the age of transaction there is a fluid, going-back-and-forth-between the different sites of knowledge and understanding. Inquiry and discovery constitute a limitless spectrum, or 'spectacle'. *Curriculum becomes continuum.*

The age of transaction may not mean the 'end of education' as we know it. Habitual structures, even amid the most tempestuous revolutions, have a strange way of abiding. But the scene of knowledge will fill most of the spaces of our lives. In the short haul the revolution at our door is about computers, browsers, connectivity with telecom systems, websites, internet relay chat, and learning with laptops instead of textbooks.

In the long haul it is about the dissolution of structures and the true freedom of the mind, a freedom that was impossible in the 'age of education'.

Chapter 6

Hypertextuality and the new terrain of liberal learning

> What we become depends on what we read after all of the professors have finished with us. The greatest university of all is a collection of books.
>
> (Thomas Carlyle)

When future chroniclers and researchers peer back at the changes presently happening in American education, the words of Dickens may be redolent with significance: 'It was the best of times, it was the worst of times'. From a broad social and economic purview the third knowledge revolution can be construed as a blessing for the professional class worldwide that historically have been known as 'educators'. Digitization of commerce and communications has transformed the so-called 'information revolution' into an explosion of both means and tasks connected with integrating aggregations of data into usable, or intelligible, systems loosely understood as 'knowledge'. Every historical invention promoting literacy, such as writing and printing, has in a certain measure had this effect.

Yet the shifts currently in progress are of an exponentially different magnitude than what has occurred in the past. If one surveys the artifacts that throughout most of history have counted as the elements, or expressions, of 'knowledge' (e.g. books, documents, broadsides, paintings, lithographs, statues, archaeological remains), then the third knowledge revolution is truly epochal, because all of these items have been swept at once into the new digital galaxy of experience.

The new system of representation

It is obvious that inordinate claims have been made, and overblown anxieties incurred, for technological shifts, in both recent and distant eras. But it is not the technological transformation that is at issue here so much as the *system of representation*. With the historical invention of each new communications medium, a different kind of representational system has been added to the repository of culture. Or the new has been largely an extension of the old.

The discovery of hieroglyphics in the Ancient Near East, and the eventual development of script, led to an expansion of the capacity of human thought and imagination that had previously been confined to oral tradition. The advent of the printing press in the fifteenth century meant that access to much of the fine art, and the whole of literature, stored in the treasury of civilization was now available to masses of people. With popular technology comes democratic politics. But these horizontal expansions of existing representational structures did not necessarily yield the kind of cognitive unification that is beginning to happen with digital culture.

The sprawling manifold we call the internet is a prima facie illustration of how this representational system appears. The internet is built on the rudimentary principle of the 'hyperlink'. And the hyperlink in principle is capable of conjoining every medium and representation of knowledge artifact, from the dialogues of Plato to the drawings of DaVinci to twentieth-century recordings of the Delta blues.[40] What pedagogical experts less than a decade ago saw as the challenge of 'connecting knowledge' by new teaching strategies and classroom coaching and mentoring is now a fact of life, when one surfs the net. The connections may be haphazard in many respects, but the addition of curricular design and expertise to the architecture of the net is producing steady improvement. When the web was new, critics most commonly complained that the most valuable educational 'content' was missing from it. That complaint has subsided as every museum, news organization, magazine, art gallery, and music library goes online. The complaint now is that it is too difficult for the student to navigate through all the options. With more intelligent search engines and subject-related 'portals' containing directories and menus of everything of importance, that sort of disquiet is likely to subside soon as well.

The representational structure that ruled the educational enterprise in the past has been *segmental* and *presentational*. In many ways, the underlying metaphor for learning has been that of the conservatory, or museum. In the conservatory the character of knowledge is shaped by the manner in which experts, curators, or 'docents' have pre-selected and framed what is 'shown' to the recipient of their services. Nothing is experienced in its rude and raw form. Everything is analysed, delimited, and finished. The most important objects of knowledge stand by themselves. They are independent items for consideration and appreciation. The advocates of so-called 'core knowledge' are ostensible partisans of this approach. A learned person is basically someone who is familiar with, and has had deep and extensive exposure, to these master icons of 'culture'. Such icons, taken together, make up what has come to be called – usually somewhat derogatorily by the critics – 'core knowledge'.[41]

Beyond the curricular wars

The so-called 'curricular wars' in higher education during the 1980s and early 1990s were essentially fought over the criteria to be used, not the process itself, of selecting what would be learned. Whether the argument concerned students reading *Hamlet* versus *The Color Purple*, or viewing David's *Liberty Leading the People* versus contemporary wooden statues handcrafted by Guatemalan peasants, the premise was always that knowledge is packaged in segmental forms that must be proffered and digested. Core knowledge is always prefabricated knowledge. Judgements concerning the validity of knowledge ultimately come down to the warrants assigned to the manufacturer.

In the transactive world warrantied knowledge constitutes one option among other configurations of knowledge. When confronted with this prospect, traditionalists are apt to howl 'relativism'. But no knowledge at any time in history has ever emerged by some kind of arbitrary procedure. Acts of selection derive from the establishment of certain cultural forms as authoritative. And these 'authorizations' in turn are founded upon certain public standards of acclamation and acceptance. Beethoven would not have become great had he not been great in his day. Even someone like the Danish philosopher Søren Kierkegaard, who was reviled and relatively obscure in his age, became famous because he 'spoke' to multitudes of a later historical generation. In the age of transaction the learner is capable of participating in the process of cultural formation. The old and dying presentational culture – the retail book industry is a good illustration – increasingly relies on pre-judgements of 'marketability' before an artifact is authorized, where markets in turn are driven by prior consensus of what is warranted. But the new digital technology creates a genuine 'free market' of culture, where taste and discernment arise, if not totally, at least in large part from direct experience of artifacts and response to them.

Cultural revolutions, as is the case in all historical revolutions, are never smooth or easy. The more the new presses on the old, the more defiant the old becomes, until there is either the solidification of reactionary forces, or the *ancien régime* finally crumbles. The *ancien régime* has won the battle from time to time when ideologies are mainly what are at stake. But the global power of digitization and network transactivity are so encompassing and awesome that the regime has absolutely no chance. It is just a matter of time before the university as we know it falls by the wayside.

The question is simply whether how mild will be the transition from the university to the hyperuniversity, from education to hyperlearning, from the command economy of knowledge to a free market in culture and knowledge. Some pundits insist that the change is actually from an artisan-based culture of learning to a 'business' model of educational delivery and distribution; but that take is short-sighted.[42] Digitization is a force that undermines industrial forms of 'corporate' organization in the same instance that it demolishes the medieval 'walled cities' of inquiry that has denoted the higher learning.

An analogy might be the revolution in retailing that took place years ago with the coming of 'superstores' or discount stores. For a time the superstore seemed poised to become dominant in retailing and replace so-called 'department stores'. But the prophets of that industry did not count on the coming of the shopping mall, which allowed for the renaissance of the small proprietor's shop in the context of a large central organization. The same will probably happen with liberal or 'artisan' learning down the road. The breadth and expansiveness of organized knowledge digital culture allows will mean a new co-operativeness and architecture of linkages between classical institutions of learning that was not possible in the past.

The general template for the new liberal learning is the hypertext, the dominant genre of present day electronic communication. George Landow, a literary theorist, has convincingly made the case that the distinctive culture of 'hypertextuality' instantiates at both a philosophical and a practical level the new digital order in the humanities. This new order, in turn, corresponds to what has been loosely defined as the 'postmodern' archetype in both learning and in scholarship. According to Landow, the reading of hypertextual materials alters the very fabric of cognitive space.

The non-linear character of hypertext also means that it is non-hierarchical. And this non-hierarchical cast signifies at once that all hypertexts are 'composed of bodies of linked texts that have no primary axis of organization'.[43] Furthermore, hypertexts also combine the pursuit of parallel, and diverging, threads of verbal information with the intuitive experience of graphic messages, pictorial configurations, and icons. According to Landow, hypertext contains visual components that are impossible within the framework of print communication. The most fundamental of these elements is the cursor, which actually allows the reader, or user, to alter the substance of the text. Unlike the practice of highlighting the texts of books and familiar print documents, electronic scholarship is 'intrusive' into the text itself. A scholar can download a text into a word processor or web publishing program, then modify it in whatever way he or she wishes. The fact that hypertexts are not only mutable, but permeable, raises profound conceptual issues, according to Landow, about what are the sorts of 'texts' we actually study in the digital environment. The reader and author are interchangeable, in the same way that in the new world of learning teacher and student are also fungible.

The text, therefore, is no longer unified as a segment of 'subject matter', but is 'dispersed' or 'disseminated' in the sense that postmodern philosophers employ the term.[44] It is not to be found in a particular 'location' or with reference to a specific author. Whereas the study of printed texts requires that one follow a narrative trajectory that is closed at both ends, hypertexts allow the reader to roam freely in any direction that seems important, or appealing. Learning neither commences nor terminates in the usual manner, but is what we might describe as 'migratory'. The migratory nature of the new learning 'creates the space of critical appreciation by deferring closure and inviting the reader/author back to the textual process over and over again, introducing with each beginning new and fresh textual perspectives'.[45]

The dispersion of texts as the rule of learning, moreover, renders as largely irrelevant the fierce debate in the 1980s over whether the texts to be studied should be part of some 'canon'. The view that texts, particularly in the humanities, can be 'canonical' originated from a comparison with the manner in which the Catholic Church prescribed what religious believers should believe during and after the Middle Ages. A canon is some officially defined, or decreed, unit of knowledge. It implies the hand of clerical authority, and the idea of 'canonical texts' was deployed by left-wing critics of traditional curriculum to suggest that what had hitherto been assumed as our common cultural heritage was in fact a peremptorily enjoined classification of knowledge. Of course, by substituting their own preferred works as part of the 'core education' process, the left wing continued to participate in the game of 'canonizing' texts. Any presumption of canonicity, however, is only possible in an educational universe where what someone reads, or ought to read, is circumscribed by the conviction of authority.

In the hypertextual setting no such bounding of what one reads is feasible. Conventional learning allows such bounding through the familiar means of instruction – textbooks, lectures, tightly arranged syllabi, and examinations aimed at evaluating how well the learner has mastered what has been already carefully prescribed. As Stephanie Gibson observes, hypertext has

> an impact on an epistemological scale larger than classroom pedagogy. It calls into question several different relationships of academic authority . . . The wider contextualization allowed by hypertext will most certainly force changes in the manner in which disciplines are conceived and expertise is attributed.[46]

Hypertextuality produces 'hyperlearning'. Hyperlearning is not 'received' from any particular source. It is constructed in craft-like fashion out of the resources available.

Hyperlearning within the hyperuniversity, therefore, transfigures the academic understanding of what constitutes a 'text'. The text is no longer an object to be analysed or assimilated. Indeed, the seemingly infinite spectrum of 'hypertextual' options the internet affords the learner renders knowledge a product of creatively combining signs and images. The common assumption that exploration of the internet amounts to mere 'surfing' reflects a prejudice that carries over from the older control structures of higher education. To the contrary, research into the habits of people who spend a large amount of time online indicates that they are decidedly purposeful in what may seem to the outside like random wandering from site to site. Online inquiry transfigures the study of texts into a broad and varied spectrum of activities. Text becomes 'texture', inasmuch as what was a previously classified range of intellectual interests now can be perceived as a more diffuse kind of adventure in cognition. The online is by its very nature *non-linear*.

An experiment in non-linear learning

I put this kind of theory to a demanding test in the spring of 1999 when I designed and taught an interdisciplinary freshman core course at the University of Denver entitled 'Word and Image in the Digital Age', or 'Wandi' as it was affectionately called. The course was planned as an experiment in teaching whatever one might teach average, or below-average, college students who would never study the humanities again everything they basically should know about the humanities as a whole. The course was part of another experimental program known as the Laptop Learning Community, or LLC. In the LLC students met their general education requirements through courses where the use of laptop computers was integral to teaching, research, and carrying through with assignments. As curricular conservatives who had fought the establishment of both the LLC and Wandi feared, the students at first seemed more interested in playing with their computers than delving into the complexities of the Russian novel, or starting to appreciate styles of modernism in art and architecture. During the past quarter the same group of students had spent ten weeks examining the sociology of 'digital culture' by participating in chatrooms and creating pseudo-identities through online forums. And they certainly appeared in no mood to take on something as down-to-basics as analysing literature. The course sequence on digital culture was a terrifying act to follow, and I met the class on the first day fully expecting to be yawned, if not booed, out of court. Miraculously, my expectations were unfounded.

My strategy in plotting out the course had been simply to offer comparisons between how one did things in the humanities in a traditional way, and how the same activity might be transposed into an electronic format. For example, the syllabus outline concentrated on the key intellectual functions that make up the humanities, such as writing, reading, interpreting texts, appreciating art, and listening to music. The students would carry through with assignments, or we would conduct exercises in class, where those functions could be accomplished both in the older manner and in the newer, digital format. We would discuss and reflect on the ways in which those functions were both similar, and different, under the contrasting circumstances. In the first segment of the course we read the contemporary 'postmodern' novel *Marabou Stork Nightmares* by Irvine Welsh, which constitutes a kind of literary hypertext in print form. We examined the structure, stylistic innovations, and character development inherent in the novel, then investigated how this postmodernist, or 'pomo', aesthetics played out electronically as well.

There was, interestingly, an unexpected historical event that fitted in incredibly, though shockingly, with the pedagogy itself. The main character in the novel resembled the pathological, adolescent personalities who carried out the shooting spree at Columbine High School in Littleton, Colorado. As it turned out, the news about the massacre broke within a few minutes after we had started class on 20 April, 1999. Immediately the class itself became a crisis scene, as every student scrambled with their laptops to go online and find up-to-the-second news and information sources that might illuminate what television and radio media were reporting.

The students themselves grasped at once the connections between art and life. The class itself had become a hypertext in which experiences flowed in and out from the 'scene' of learning itself. All the modalities of the world wide web – text, graphics, sound, multimedia – were mustered simultaneously to define intellectually an 'event' that was not only contemporary 'news', but in some sense a literary performance. When students wrote their mid-term examinations – online – they comprehended at once the kind of nonliterary educational experience they had undergone. Many students had done their own research both on the author and his artistry of the English working class. They had also investigated the youthful 'Goth' subculture in which Harris and Klebold were allegedly steeped, then drew them together into essays that made sense out of both the text itself, and the text of culture.

The next course segment involved study of visual culture, particularly in its electronic manifestations. Instead of taking the 'survey' approach that is commonplace in the humanities, we focused on a simple set of artifacts, a group of paintings by the French surrealist painter René Magritte. Magritte's art is perplexing and beguiling. Every painting is a kind of rebus, or brain-teaser. Meticulously designed images or symbols clash on the canvas, or are so strange and paradoxical they cause pereceptual convulsions. A face becomes a breast, a translucent and celestial sky intrudes into a dark and sinister crime scene. Each painting can be construed as a kind of ocular hypertext that compels the viewer to move back and forth in many directions, resulting in the discernment of a different configuration of 'meaning' with each pass of the eye, much as in the twisting of a kaleidoscope. In order to set the inquiry of the students in motion, I offered an online 'lecture', which can be described as a concise, but somewhat elliptical, set of statements about Magritte and art. The 'lecture' was posted in the web forum, and students were assigned the task of responding to the text, to each other, and to the body of knowledge that loomed beyond the periphery of their awareness in the online universe. What I discovered very quickly was that the principle of hypertextual 'reading' was not restricted to whatever the students did whenever they logged on. It had become on the main a whole new genre of learning, and hence of cognition. Orthogonal, or non-linear, cognition is something the traditional university is not prepared for. What the course 'experiment' in a modest way demonstrated to me is that the concept of 'hypertext' defines the new directionality of 'hyperlearning', which in turn points toward the formation of the hyperuniversity.

Furthermore, in the digital environment there is a whole new 'hyperspace' of learning, which by the same token generates a nonsequential and multi-directional synthesis of sensation, imagination, and intellectual activity. We call this synthesis 'hyperexperience', which comes remarkably close to the theories of how the Prussian philosopher Kant two centuries ago claimed we come to 'know' what we know. Writing in German, Kant had used the term *Vielfältigkeit*, or 'manifoldness'. Literally the word can be translated as 'many-sidedness', and implies the non-linearity of knowledge itself. Kant's whole career as a philosopher was devoted to refuting what we might describe as the 'scientism' and 'logicism' of traditional philosophy by arguing, often in very complex and abstruse discourse, that reason, feeling, and moral sentiments altogether constitute legitimate types of experience in their own right. Each type of experience amounts to a peculiar synthesis, or 'judgement' in Kant's phrasing.

My point is not that Kant anticipated the internet. Kantian philosophy is far richer and intricate than any comparison with the 'digital landscape' might brook. But conventional American education with its own kind of rote presentation and pervasive scientism is finding itself between a rock and a hard place in the digital revolution. Conventional education with its sequential 'grade' system, its pre-requisites and course sequences, and its hierarchical understanding of how knowledge is created is completely out-of-sync with the digital mindscape itself. This new kind of dysfunctionality between education in its dominant institutional forms and the processes of experience and learning has been bearable so long as there was a rigid barrier between the 'world' and the classroom. However, the pervasive nature of non-linear perception that is integral to our habits of 'on-linearity' must inevitably alter our learning institutions in the same way that a constant battering of hurricane tides will rapidly change the coastline.

Because on-linearity implies the loss of authorization, it is likely that scholars, pedagogues, and bureaucrats will not easily accept the changes that are in store. We are not talking about the sudden closure of traditional universities, although that scenario has been a form of apocalyptic wishful thinking in recent years among the more trendy company of digerati. A useful analogy might be the way in which suburban and older urban neighbourhoods have developed in the postwar era. The explosion of suburban sprawl in the 1950s and 1960s for a while left the old inner city decrepit and decaying. But in less than a generation 'gentrification' set in, whereby many of the cultural values prized by denizens of the urban scene combined with the esthetic qualities and upscale lifestyles that people had earlier sought in the suburbs. Traditional universities are likely to experience over time a similar form of 'digital gentrification' which will preserve the comfortable and intimate sense of a residential campus with the 'global reach' of digital communications. The same will be true of instruction in the liberal arts. Distance learning on the internet can never suffice for the direct experience of viewing a masterpiece by Van Gogh or Mondrian in New York's Museum of Modern Art. Nor can it ever offer the aesthetic enjoyment of carefully poring through a 'great book' with marginal glosses and appended commentary. These modes of intellectual experience will always continue with the treasured status accorded by a specific elite. But just as monastic or clerical schools gradually gave way under the pressures of industrialism to comprehensive universities, so those universities with their organizations resembling the manufacturing facilities of nineteenth-century urban societies will melt into the 'extramural' and electronically distributed learning spaces of the digital century.

The shift will not be easy. As Baker, Hale and Gifford comment sardonically about the new 'digital curriculum' under construction in the higher learning, 'it is easier to "bolt-on" CMI [computer mediated instructional] materials to traditional teaching environments than to reconceptualize the entire teaching and learning enterprise for a relatively small amount of curriculum materials'.[47]

The slow pace cannot be justified in terms of maintaining educational 'quality'.

> Compared with students enrolled in conventionally taught courses, students who are provided regular access to well-crafted computer-mediated instructional (CMI) materials generally achieve higher scores on summary examinations (improved learner effectiveness), learn their lessons in less time (increased learner efficiency), like their classes more (greater learner engagement) and develop more positive attitudes toward the discipline under inquiry (enhanced learner interest). These results hold for a broad range of students, stretching from elementary to college students, studying across a broad range of disciplines, from mathematics to the social sciences to the humanities. The findings also hold for students who vary greatly in terms of their prior knowledge, educational experiences, preferences for particular types of instructional assistance and English language proficiency.[48]

The inherent conservatism, if not the reactionary tenor, of residential university faculty, however, cannot be blithely appeased without major costs, both in terms of the value of education and the ethics of its delivery. A strong, moral imperative to build the hyperuniversity emerges out of the digital culture itself. According to Ray Steele, 'We cannot teach students in the environment of an 1856 classroom and then expect them to go and be successful in an electronic world'.[49] Another moral argument derives from the fundamental axiology of liberal arts education itself. The prime justification for liberal learning in the twentieth century has been the exposure of the hitherto parochial and youthful mind to claims and perspectives that would not ordinarily arise in the natural course of personal development. In the now antiquated rhetoric of liberal studies this precept was articulated as 'broadening horizons'. Today it is usually cast as 'promoting diversity'. At the same time, many teachers in the liberal arts, who have handily embraced the teaching of cultural pluralism while clenching fiercely their authoritarian privileges in the classroom, fail to see the hypocrisy of their own stance. Digital pedagogy furthers quite radically the ideal of forcing the student to encounter 'otherness' in the realm of both knowledge and experience. It puts them in play with many other individuals 'who belong to numerous discourse communities'.[50] Exposing students to a plurality of discourse communities populating the global electronic agora, even non-academic ones, is just as critical to the 'liberalizing' and 'humanizing' process of general education as teaching about slave narratives, or introducing students to Hindu temple rituals. In the unbounded planet of textuality that is electronic hypertext discourse communities interpenetrate and fuse in ways that have never been possible before in human history. The scholarly community, although it constantly gives lip service to the maxims of openness, pluralism, and democracy, is very often terrified of letting its own discourse community be challenged by popular styles of communication. But this challenge cannot be averted. In the same manner as the printing press powered the reformation of the Church in the sixteenth century by shattering the caste control of reading by the clergy, the ubiquity of hypertext is already impelling a reformation of the academy by undermining the hegemony of the 'knowledge specialist'.

The reversal of authority

The redefinition in the postmodern era of authority and authorization can never be reversed. Such a redefinition lies at the heart of what we are beginning to understand as the 'postmodern condition' itself. Indeed, the new archetype of the liberal arts that digital technology proffers can be described as 'postmodernist' in the fullest sense of the word.[51] That is because hypertextuality entails the radical, and in principle, infinite expansion of knowledge space itself. Whereas for millennia knowledge was 'enclosed' (i.e. it was localized within the topographies of museums, castles, monasteries, libraries, book binderies, and even film archives), today its architecture is uncircumscribable. One 'thread' of information may crystallize in a lead or hunch, then generate many parallel linkages within the vast cyberuniverse that continue to generate 'realizations' that are not necessarily 'conclusions' or 'ideas'. The dynamic nature of knowledge, of course, was anticipated in the movement of nineteenth-century philosophy known as German idealism, of which Hegel was the critical exemplar. But this dynamism, which Hegel himself somewhat mystically named 'Spirit', can now be discerned as a concrete phenomenon in the world-encompassing digital society. Hegel refused to let knowledge be broken down and sequestered within tight, scholarly cubicles. In his major writings he employed a fluid kind of philosophical rhetoric to show how themes in art, culture, religion, literature, and political thought were constantly interpenetrating and moving in some grand tidal flow toward new heights of fusion and synthesis. The workings of the world wide web may not yet approximate what Hegel termed the 'philosophy of absolute spirit'. But metaphorical shadowings of this process are unavoidable.

The liberal arts themselves were forged in a Medieval environment where the ancient Greek science of distinction and classification ruled along with the authoritarian regime of philosophy and theology. The original prototype of the university itself reflects this type of intellectual governance. As Nathan Schachner notes, 'the university was peculiarly a Medieval invention'.[52] Furthermore, from the founding of the university 'the principle of authority was made a fetish. Aristotle and the Bible were sacrosanct; so were the Church Fathers . . . Whatever was written in these volumes was holy, not to be questioned or investigated or changed by the tiniest jot. All knowledge was fixed and known in so far as it would ever be given to man to know'.[53] Though the modern idea of self-development and free inquiry has at least nominally been accepted over the years by the academy, the principle of authority and hierarchy has not yet eroded.

It is no longer the Church and its canon jurists who determine what knowledge is 'fixed'. It is departments and curriculum committees. The Medieval conviction of *nulla salus extra ecclesiam* ('there is no salvation outside the church') has been replaced by *nulla cognitio extra universitatem* ('there is no knowledge outside the university'). The effect is no different.

Chapter 7

Postmodernist premises

> Our working hypothesis is that the status of knowledge is altered as societies enter what is known as the postindustrial age and culture enters what is known as the postmodern age.
>
> (Jean François Lyotard)

With the coming of the postmodern university, or hyperuniversity, however, the Medieval walls of the academy can barely stand. Advanced learning is without question entering the postmodern age. But what do we mean by 'postmodern' in the more broad-ranging, philosophical use of the term? And what are the implications of this philosophical world view for the future of digital learning itself?

The terms 'postmodern' and 'postmodernism' have been swatted about the air in recent years like so many bright-coloured beach balls. Whereas all but mossbacks among social theorists concur that the postmodern era with its fluid definitions of personal identity, nationhood, culture, and knowledge has arrived in force, the models of instruction and inquiry that govern most of what we know as higher education are decidedly Medieval, let alone modern. The *status quo* cannot be maintained much longer. The question is not whether higher education is going to undergo a transformation. The only question is how soon it will occur, and how stressful the change will be.

It is not our business to speculate on the details of institutional transformation. The more entrenched any cultural institution is, the more it has the capacity to hang together with a mysterious tensile strength. But what we can do is begin to envision the basic 'architectural' principles of the new hyperlearning as it spreads throughout the educational ambience. Contrary to digital determinists who take the view that technological mandates have most to do with what ultimately happens, our view is simply that digital learning and digital technology in the educational setting develop according to the same topography as the culture at large. As is true of all cultural institutions in transition, there may be a time lag between what takes place on the broader scene and what actually occurs in the 'classroom' and in the recently refurbished learning spaces. But the lag is not indefinite. The 'postmodern condition', as Lyotard has denoted it, is our condition. The remaining issue is how we can comfortably describe learning under postmodern conditions, which are at once the same that define digital culture overall.

The benchmarks of postmodernist thought

Although no contemporary philosopher has yet mapped out a typology of postmodern thought forms and practices, the following scheme may apply to what we are indeed considering.

First, postmodern philosophy is characterized by a refusal to ground what we know in certain unshakable 'positions' on which all understanding rests. Technically speaking, this refusal constitutes what such philosophers call the 'overcoming of the metaphysical'. All metaphysical systems of representation throughout Western history, from Aristotle to Hegel, have rested on the notion that there were certain conceptual anchors (what the Greeks knew as *archai*, or 'first principles') from which all hypotheses and inferences could be adduced. These first principles were at first logical and scientific. But by the Middle Ages they had become 'theological' – in short, they referred to some transcendent point of orientation beyond the spectrum of everyday perception and experience. Because the *archai* could not be experienced, or even conceptualized, directly, they could only be articulated by ancient, or clerical, authorities.

With the decline of religious authority in the seventeenth and eighteenth centuries, these first principles came to be grasped once more as rational and self-sufficient truths. Philosophical and scientific authorities replaced theological ones. Theologian Paul Lakeland notes that postmodernism in large measure amounts to a 'breakdown of what have previously been taken to be "givens", fundamental co-ordinates of experience. The givens in question are time, space, and order. Postmodernity puts each of these three into question, both collapsing and then expanding the understanding of each'.[54]

As we have seen, the space of traditional university learning is hierarchical, or 'laddered', space. Hierarchy was the rudimentary analogue for all systems of order from classical times until at least the turn of the twentieth century. Knowledge space, like social space, and like the space of the cathedrals and palaces that comprised the political and cultural context of life itself, could be mapped on a vertical axis. Knowledge 'emanated' from above, from an authoritative apex. Learning was not initiated, it was received. Teachers, administrators, trustees, and governors all could be fitted squarely into this hierarchical space.

But, as Lyotard points out, 'the status of knowledge is altered as societies enter what is known as the postindustrial age and cultures enter what is known as the postmodern age'.[55] Though Lyotard is writing before the advent of the personal computer and networked communications, his insights have been confirmed by the new social contours carved out by digital technology. 'Knowledge', Lyotard says, 'in general cannot be reduced to science, not even to learning'.[56] Postmodern knowledge he describes as 'competence', or 'performativity', as opposed to 'narrative'. Narrativity suffuses hierarchy. The 'way things' are is told time and time again. Every 'discipline' from psychology to history has a 'tradition' of thinkers and practitioners behind it that is repeated and iterated anew for each successive generation.

But the 'performance' principle reveals a new set of institutional relationships that subsist not only within the university itself, but in the relationship of the university to the culture. The role of the university now is to improve the functioning of the knowledge operations, as opposed to the transmission of a stock of knowledge itself, which come from within the society itself.

> Knowledge will no longer be transmitted *en bloc*, once and for all, to young people before their entry into the work force: rather it is and will be served 'a la carte' to adults who are either working or expect to be, for the purpose of improving their skills and chances of promotion, but also to help them acquire information, languages, and language games allowing them both to widen their occupational horizons and to articulate their technical and ethical experience.[57]

Whereas narrativity implies standards and criteria established in past generations of scholarship, performativity suggests the opposite. 'A postmodern artist or writer', Lyotard declares, 'is in the position of a philosopher: the text he writes, the work he produces are not in principle governed by preestablished rules, and they cannot be judged according to a determining judgement, by applying familiar categories to the text or the work.'[58]

Hypertextuality's 'strange geometry'

In translating Lyotard's characterization of the postmodern into digital learning theory, we realize at once that the 'strange' geometry of a hypertextual textuality means that the rules for the production of knowledge have to be invented as we move through the matrix of the new knowledge space. Contemporary social theory carries on about the social 'construction' of knowledge. But in the digital epoch the act of construction is not by any means a collective gesture. Nor is it an independent and arbitrary move of the individual 'knowledge player'. The new knowledge space of the postmodern university is a latticework of learner-motivated inquiries and strategies that follow along with the expertise of the knowledge professional – what heretofore we have known as the 'teacher' or 'professor'. The lattice is interwoven with the territory of the culture. It is a permeable space. It is a liberated space. It is knowledge that has outstripped its fetal form as 'formal' teaching and research.

The problem is similar to the one of Geoffrey Nunberg in his essay entitled 'Farewell to the information age' on the transmogrification of periodical publishing by the internet. Nunberg makes the point that the myth of the 'information age', which antedates personal computing, coincides with late industrialism and the rise of mass consumer culture. The very notion of 'information' implies a basic consumer mentality. Information 'providers' serve up what ordinary people need in order to be 'informed'. Information in an important sense becomes simply another commodity manufactured for a mass market.

The analogy, of course, derives from the corporate culture of the entertainment industry. Information is something to be passively encountered, though not engaged or assimilated. Information allows for a certain temporary 'enjoyment', but it is not something that can be wrestled with, analysed, and critically refracted. Although philosophers and literary theorists have talked for generations about the strategies and interventions for critically 'reading' a text, the opportunities for hermeneutical insight do not necessarily arise even in a culture of mass literacy. In the world of book-based 'information' most knowledge is something that is simply presented. People take at face value what they read and do not interrogate the information as they go along. Ironically, the fact that books are generated by authors, who can only publish if they can be certified as 'authorities' in some sense on their topic area, means that the critical response of the reader is usually weak, and frequently non-existent.

The situation is quite different with the readily accessible, easily published, hyperlinked 'information' that comprises the internet. Nunberg writes that 'on the Web . . . you can never have the kind of experience that you can have with the information genres of print, the experience of interpreting a text simply *as* a newspaper or encyclopedia article without attending to its author, its publisher, or the reliability of its recommender'. He goes on to say:

> We read Web documents, that is, not as information but as intelligence, which requires an explicit warrant of one form or another. Sometimes this is provided by a masthead that announces that the document has been produced by a well-known organization or print publication, in which case the content of the document does indeed constitute a kind of derivative information. With primary electronic documents, though, the warrant more often comes, as with the intelligence of old, from sources whose reliability we can judge from personal experience.[59]

What Nunberg is actually saying should come as quite a shock to curricular conservatives in the academy. He is suggesting that the preconfiguration of 'knowledge' by academic specialists through the process of direct transmission (as opposed to transactivity) does not nurture the time-honoured curricular goals of independent reasoning and investigation, but militates against them. At the same time, that observation seems intuitively correct. Still at the dawn of the third millennium the higher education system, despite its modernist pretensions about emancipating the mind from habit and convention, is still stuck inside the chain mail and armour of its Medieval progenitor. Authority, not free inquiry, is the dominant and seemingly insurmountable norm in the classroom. The traditional lecture and course text, not to mention the lockstep scheduling of classes and classrooms, are the seal of this heretofore immutable method of creating knowledge. There is a postmodern mind emerging that remains torturously confined within the adamantine dungeons of a pre-modern administrative system. This contradiction cannot endure much longer.

Postmodern philosophical thought offers a rationale for the freeing of the mind that the modern university has to date tended to shackle. What Nunberg calls 'intelligence', or what might be better called 'critical intelligence', can only come about as part of an educational strategy that allows the 'learner' to wander in what might be otherwise considered a wilderness of 'unauthorized' documents and sources. If the postmodern intellectual nomad is not to perish in the wilderness, he or she must learn the skills of engagement. He or she must master the means of achieving competency. A typical cavil concerning 'learner-directed learning' is that it is fine for working adults, but inappropriate for adolescent students who do not have the maturity or the self-possession to take responsibility for their own education. Even though colleges and universities have abandoned strict moral safeguards for their clientele, the rule of 'in loco parentis' still holds sway ideologically and is used to legitimate what are in effect high-priced habits of diverting students from the serious business of intellectual engagement. More and more of escalating tuition dollars on 'residential' campuses are not flowing in the direction of raising performance standards, but of finding new ways of augmenting the socialization process, which is already the prevailing component in traditional learning environments.

Artifacts and signs

The development of critical intelligence depends on a growing understanding of the correlation between artifacts and signs. Dewey dimly recognized the importance of this relationship in his philosophy of education, but the subtlety was lost in his often incontinent prose and the misapplication of his theories by 'progressive' educational reformers in the early and mid-twentieth century. Postmodern philosophy, which derives from a radical new conception of language and meaning, enables us to go where Dewey was incapable of going. Much of postmodern thought has been built upon so-called 'post-structuralist' linguistic theory, which is most closely associated with the extensive works of the French philosopher Jacques Derrida. It is not within our scope to go over in any detail the contributions of Derrida, which are difficult for the layperson to comprehend. But we can make a few synoptic observations that are germane to our approach.

In his early writings Derrida talks about meaning and significance as acts of 'deconstruction'. What Derrida originally intended by the term 'deconstruction' has very little to do with what the phrase has come to connote in popular culture and among reactionary critics. It does not mean the 'destruction' of culture, moral relativism, or nihilism. It refers strictly to the anthropological consideration that the 'object' which a word or an image signifies is not something either conceptually or materially obvious. Post-structuralist theory, which goes back to pioneering work of French linguist Ferdinand de Saussure, rests on the discovery that words as signs do not signify 'things', but rather other signs.

Furthermore, Saussure noted that one sign implies another sign not by 'pointing' to it in the same way that one can demonstrate to a child what the word 'dog' means by directing attention to a furry, four-legged animal that barks and pants. Signs imply each other by 'differentiation', according to Saussure. Thus the statement 'that dog Rover is a hairy hound' signifies in identifying a creature by showing discrepancies between hounds that are hairy and hounds that are not. The 'significance' of the proper name Rover can be ascertained by differentiating between the two kinds of hounds. Derrida enlarges upon this straightforward principle in making the case that philosophy does not deal with 'the real world', but with the world of emblems, allusions, and methods of signification, including writing, painting, and other communications media. Demonstrating the 'spaces', the gaps, the nullities, or moments of 'difference' that shade between signifying items, or instruments, is how we arrive at both meaning and understanding. That is what in a nutshell Derrida has been driving toward all these years with the much misunderstood idea of 'deconstruction'. A deconstructed text is but a transparent one.

While Derrida has concentrated mainly on writing and 'grammatical' means of representation, the postmodernist principle of 'deconstructed' textuality has increasingly been applied to written, visual, and even auditory sign systems. Sign systems themselves can be means of differentiation and moments of deconstruction.

For example, the Magritte's painting is gaining increasing attention because of the way in which he creates a sense of mystery or
puzzlement by imposing incongruous images, or images and texts.
One of his most famous works shows the pictorial representation
of a pipe with the enigmatic inscription *ceci ne pas un pipe* ('This
is not a pipe').[60] The inscription counters the image and creates a
baffling disjunction in the mind of the viewer, but it also calls attention to a semantic fact overlooked by common sense. The pipe and
the representation of the pipe are not the same thing. Moreover, the
'pipe' supposedly represented is in itself a pictorial representation,
which one could naively describe in words as a 'pipe', if the words
themselves did not underscore the gaping chasm of differentiation
between the visual and the verbal. The Magritte painting in itself
is tantamount to a kind of 'multi-media' essay on the arbitrary
nature of the sign. And this ensemble of perceptual paradoxes and
discrepancies forces the viewer of the painting into a higher-order
kind of critical analysis that is not possible when one merely looks
at a picture, reads a book, or listens to an orchestral piece.

The hypertextual richness of the internet, in which all forms of
media and signifying instrumentalities converge, makes the intellectual challenge of the web something like a Magritte painting. When
detractors carp about the 'low quality' of unauthorized web content,
they are concentrating only on the spurious comparison of the
internet to old forms of 'infotainment' media. They are ignoring
the intellectual challenge to the 'internaut' of conquering complex,
cognitive space. According to Jay Bolter, 'Web documents are experiments in the integration of visual and verbal communication. The
hypertextual character of these documents – the fact that text,
graphics, and video may be linked electronically – defines a space
in which arbitrary signs can coexist with perceptual presentation'.
In the same breath, he adds, the coexistence is not 'peaceful'. 'The
verbal text must now struggle to assert its legitimacy in a space
dominated by visual modes of representation.'[61]

The new knowledge space

This new space is what we may refer to generically as 'postmodern
knowledge space'. Postmodern knowledge space is a sort of multi-
modal, hypertextual 'hyperspace'. It is an illimitable space laid out
through a network of signifying relations that are the same time a
texture of 'contextualities', a web of *ligatures and differences*. Post-

modern knowledge space is to the traditional classroom-and-instructor-defined space as our vision of outer space today is to the Ptolemaic space of the Middle Ages. The hyperuniversity with its new pedagogy of hyperlearning is the charter school for the exploration of this knowledge space. As the internet as a technological invention loses its fascination to futurists and social visionaries, the intellectual possibilities of an ever-expanding 'content-rich' space for intellectual colonization will start to incite the imagination. One of the reasons the internet has not captivated the company of serious intellectuals is that intellectuals themselves, so transfixed by their ancient seigneurial rights in the Medieval system of instruction, have not for the most part discerned the vast prospects for 'intelligence' coming from the use of the web.

Digital intelligence is a strange and forbidding form of hyper-intelligence that cannot be controlled by the seigneurial system. The commercialization of the web and its swift conversion from an electronic village populated by *au courant* techies to an immense virtual shopping mall has impaired this trend in the short run. In the long haul, however, a certain realization will set in that the simple 'convenience' of gathering information, corresponding with friends and associates, and shopping on the internet is overshadowed by the exchange of ideas and the integration of experience with higher-grade reflection that is the prime ingredient in what we optimally know as 'education'.

Exploring the internet will then become the voyage of discovery it was envisioned to be a decade ago. The way in which the internet has become the central conduit for communication among scholars themselves testifies to these possibilities. The transactivity that is already flourishing among knowledge specialists has not passed onto the realm of interaction between professionals and students only because the specialists themselves, either out of lethargy, anxiety, or ignorance, have refused to change their way of doing things. If it were not for tenure and accrediting agencies, which jealously reinforce the old ways, the change might have happened much more swiftly.

Digital intelligence feeds on the explosion of heterogeneity. 'Heterogeneity' has become something of a cliché in the post-modernist idiom. The postmodernist sensibility compasses the play of differences, the constant subdivision of cellular units of significance into new and fruitful combinations. Differentiation, therefore, is a kinetic process. Gliding from one filament to another in the jagged, but interstitched tapestry of information makes the student aware of the countless lesions and disjunctions that cause one to query and to ponder. The heterogeneous knowledge space of the postmodern university is an open space. It is a space of infinite spacings and tracings. The university itself is an open university.

The example of Britain's Open University

Great Britain's Open University (OU), founded in 1971, is a pioneering venture in the transition to the postmodernist model. The OU is the UK's largest university with enrolments of over 200,000 'students and customers', as its advertisement states, in 1997–8. Furthermore, it takes in more than a fifth of all part-time post-secondary students in the British Isles.[62] It is ranked among the leading universities in Britain for the excellence of its teaching. Courses are not just offered within the UK, but across Europe, and recently the Open University has developed 'partnering' programmes in America as well. 'Open' also means open admissions. There are no entrance requirements. Nevertheless, the university boasts that 70 per cent of all students finish their course work each year.

Approximately 40,000, or about a fifth of the total student body, conducts its studies through interactive technologies and in online formats. Over 62,000 use computers routinely in their courses. The university has created an electronic conferencing system called FirstClass, which permits students from about 150 different courses to take part in discussion forums where messages are shown to everyone involved. Many students hand in their assignments by means of email or web pages. Tutors receive the assignments through a web interface and grade them, then return them to the students through the same medium. Grades are automatically recorded in a student's university assessment record.

The Open University's stab at what educational theorists have dubbed 'distributed learning' is only a beginning, and the available hardware and software power per student is probably not even of the same magnitude as at many top-tier institutions. Yet the Open University seems to have implemented a broad institutional learning design setup that is congruent with the architecture of global networked communications. Many institutions, particularly old-guard liberal arts institutions, are merely wiring up students and classrooms without much attention to the disparity between their familiar residential learning spaces and the new vistas of knowledge space the internet brings forth. Giving every student a laptop computer and broadband internet access without repatterning the space of the mind itself is in many ways a baroque monstrosity. Such high-ticket, high tech educational experiences are highly cost-inefficient, as well as intellectually pretentious. The Open University, on the other hand, has achieved some of the more utopian aspirations of the digital age at a fraction of the cost. As we shall see, institutions such as the Open University that began with an eye to teaching students 'any time any where' have found it easier to adapt to what popular writer Jeremy Rifkin has called the 'age of access'.[63] The age of access is a stormy petrel for the West's intellectual elites. For it confronts on a whole new scale the claim of the captains of the knowledge industry to enjoy sovereign rights against the knowledge workers themselves.

The politics of postmodernism

Postmodern theory is not entirely comfortable with digital society. A form of 'political postmodernism', particularly evident in the writings of Frederic Jameson, boils down to the transference of the language of Marxism into the new philosophical idiom. The political postmodernists continue to view technology as a tool of what Jameson calls 'late capitalism', while recounting the alleged manner in which computerization augments the power of large-scale corporate interests.[64] Indeed, the new digital technology has become an arena for the sparring of giant business empires, as the Microsoft anti-trust proceedings have shown. And the effort of such empires to co-opt the digital revolution in the name of 'corporate training' while promulgating more and more 'business' approaches to education would certainly seem to support Jameson's contention.

A popular book published in the mid-1990s by Stan Davis and Jim Botkin made the unabashed case that the new technologies would eventuate in the confluence throughout society of business and educational practices. Davis and Botkin insist that the adoption of technology by familiar educational institutions is nothing more than an attempt to 'automate the past'. According to these authors, the technological revolution is fomenting a 'redefinition' of education itself that is post-institutional. The functions of education will eventually be taken up by profit-motivated and market-savvy commercial enterprises.

Information technologies become involved in delivering education directly, on network strings and through computer cans,
without going through schools . . . Schools are also being
replaced by suppliers such as publishing and entertainment
industries and by distributors such as phone and cable companies. Information technologies are integrating value chains,
displacing links that aren't contributing adequately, and causing
players all along the chain to access the customer directly.[65]

That trend, however, is no more apparent today than it was in
1994.

The common flaw in Jameson's thinking as well as in the vision of
Davis and Botkin is that they are economic determinists without any
deeper appreciation of how the structures of technology and the
space of cognition interact with each other. Although educational
institutions as we know them may eventually disappear, and 'education' in the commonplace sense of the term may become a sheltered
relic of an industrial past, the sphere of human behaviour where
what we know, or think we know, is constantly disrupted by new
knowledge that underscores what we have not yet known, will
persist in distinguishable forms. Educational culture has always
been a burr in the saddle of consumer culture. Both enthusiasts for
the new capitalism and its post-Marxist derogators wrongly regard
the new technology as an aid to enhancing the authority of corporate
power elites. The economic successes of the entrepreneurs of the so-
called 'new economy' may succour this illusion. But the technology
itself is something more than a sword in the hands of corporate, or
bureaucratic, samurai. Its anti-authoritarian nature must lead to the
democratization of the learning polity for the new century. And this
process of democratization is propelled by the fluidity of the very
tokens of knowledge itself in the digital age.

Jameson himself has defined history as 'what hurts'. What will
hurt for educators of all stripes in this new historical interval is the
recognition that the task of the educator is to let go of many of the
privileges he has so carefully shepherded and prized down through
the centuries.

Chapter 8

The global university

> Knowledge is of two kinds: we know a subject ourselves, or we know where we can find information upon it.
>
> (Samuel Johnson)

The postmodern university, which we have called the hyper-university, is at the same time *a global university*. In the past two decades or more social and economic visionaries have encouraged us to 'think globally'. The globalization of the market economy, which accelerated with the collapse of the Berlin Wall in 1989 and the fall of the Soviet Union in 1991, is now a *fait accompli*, even though the trend has provoked cries and alarms in different political quarters, even in the Western world. But the globalization of commerce would have been impossible without the development of a worldwide technological infrastructure of digital communications that has facilitated the rapid flow of data and information, especially in the arena of financial services. At the same time the accelerating transfers of information have fostered the conditions for the first time in history for what might be termed a 'global knowledge base'. Theoreticians of digital culture have imagined the internet itself as a vast, electronic library with unlimited reserves and universal access. But ideal and reality are still worlds apart from each other. One of the central reasons for this persistent disconnection is the tendency of publishers to withhold high-quality documents from electronic distribution systems because of the logistical difficulty of charging customers and the ethos of free information that has dominated the internet since its inception. Research libraries at the same time have not offered public access to electronic documents because of copyright restrictions. So the utopia of global information sharing remains a distant, if not inconceivable, prospect.

Yet the new global knowledge space is slowly becoming defined, if only at an embryonic level. Although the oligopoly power of traditional educational institutions in the developed world, as well as force of habit, has kept electronic course delivery and formats from breaking free of their 'experimental' and marginal curricular status, in the Third World an entirely different scenario is emerging. Indeed, outside the advanced economies of the West, the internet is speeding a planetary revolution in learning. The mandate, if not yet the actuality, is implied in a statement by the Netscape corporation, which first engineered the graphics user interface that opened up the internet. Netscape sees itself as furnishing 'global education enterprise solutions' along with a 'global learning infrastructure for education communities'. The internet itself, according to Netscape, will lay the groundwork for 'networked global partnerships' involving learning centres, industry specialists, and publishers along a broad spectrum.[66]

Globalization 'from below'

The digital revolution is a movement that Alice K. Johnson calls 'globalization from below'. According to Johnson, 'the main aim of globalization from below is to establish a clear global agenda, with global structures, but with the initiative taken by ordinary people'.[67] Johnson cites the 'E-mail Partnership Project' for which the author received funding to set up regular cross-cultural interchanges between American and Romanian students. Although a programme of email swapping might on the face of it be considered as little more than a high-tech version of student 'pen pals', Johnson points out that the programme was extremely effective and valuable in promoting cross-cultural understanding. Text-based email is actually a high-powered instructional tool, inasmuch as the lack of visual perception of the person with whom one is in contact offers 'a more neutral, communication ground'. This neutral ambience makes it possible for students to come to experience each other without the intimidating or divisive sorts of non-verbal cues signifying cultural differences, which face-to-face encounters can engender.

Yet the electronic classroom has also raised the stakes for education as a whole everywhere in the world. In the international setting if e-learning 'were not available, little learning would take place', write a group of educators who have done case studies of distance learning in developing countries. 'Distance learning is often the only viable alternative when there is a paucity of technical talent, lack of funds, or extraordinary distances and isolation in areas of a country.'[68] Developing nations spend less than a tenth per students on education than do developed countries. And internet-based learning modalities are often the only option. In Honduras, for example, such a simple remote instructional device as interactive radio has resulted in 'sharp increases in student achievement'.[69] Outside the United States 'distance universities' have grown at a phenomenal pace. Whereas American higher education still strives to follow elite models, the electronic classroom in the Third World has become an effective instrument of democratization. Distance institutions, according to Empire State University president James Hall, 'confront, as do few other institutions, the often conflicting claims of educational access and intellectual achievement'. They are becoming a 'major force of change' across the spectrum of the higher learning.[70]

The internet as a learning medium is compelling change even in conservative Islamic countries, where the education of women has been held back by severe strictures of religious orthodoxy. At the Prince Hussein Information Technology Community Center in Safaw, Jordan women learn to use personal computers and enrol in distance education courses that are sponsored by the government. Because Islamic custom does not allow them to travel to attend school on their own, they can reap the benefits of a college education by online exposure. The men can study the latest techniques for livestock breeding as well as consult Arabic language web sites that range over many topics from religion to poetry to health matters.[71] A number of studies have shown that electronic education, including satellite uplinks, may prove to be the leavening agent that Muslim societies, particularly those with burgeoning populations and high illiteracy rates, desperately require. It can also, as Jamal al-Sharhan observes, satisfy the 'cultural imperative in many Muslim countries of segregating male and female students, which is often difficult to provide in remote areas'.[72]

Beyond the cultural particularities of higher education

The makeup of the global university, therefore, both accommo-dates and transcends spatial barriers as well as cultural oppositions. Purists and conventionalists may argue that 'real education' can only occur in a direct, face-to-face environment, which is indeed wholly local. But the empirical evidence increasingly indicates that what counts as the 'higher learning' is taking place routinely apart from the physical classroom. Africa especially is fertile soil for this enter-prise. Because economic and social circumstances inhibit the wide-spread construction of the typical, bricks-and-mortar Western university throughout Africa, the notion of reaching the continent's undereducated masses through virtual methods of instruction is rapidly gaining interest. A new organization called the African Distance Learning Association (ADLA) has been responsible in large part for the creation of the new Africa Virtual University (AVU). The AVU was launched by the World Bank under its InfoDev initiative. It has become a $1.2 million project that relies primarily on satellite linkages with telephone voice hookups in the English-speaking nations of Kenya, Ghana, Ethiopa, Tanzania, Uganda, Namibia, and Zimbabwe. Facilities using the French as well as the Portuguese languages are also planned. The curriculum, devoted primarily to electrical engineering, mathematics, and physics, has been developed in Europe and the United States. Instructional format includes both videotapes and live lectures that are enhanced with internet content and interactivity. The World Bank has delivered hundreds of computers to participating sites around Africa.[73]

AVU has also been critical throughout Africa in overcoming gender barriers to education, as have similar ventures in the Middle East. AVU has conducted leadership programmes for Africa women in conjunction with the Centre for International Private Enterprise using remote sites in the different nations whose constitu-encies it serves. The goal of the programme has been to mobilize Africa women for personal engagement and the sharing of learning experiences through advanced technology. It has also endeavoured to facilitate economic growth. Research on developing nations demonstrates that those which empower women through educa-tional opportunities perform far better in the global emporium while raising standards of living. As Etienne Baranshamaje, AVU founder, is often quoted as saying: 'The true barrier to progress is mindset. AVU innovation is not about technology or academic content. It is about pedagogy and human resources practices'.

While digital communications have significantly augmented the job of nation-building through the elaboration of relatively low-cost educational infrastructure, they have also improved the quality of church missions projects, where education and training have always gone hand in hand with evangelism. Global University, based in Springfield, Missouri, serves as a worldwide distributor of distance learning content for missionaries in over 160 countries and 130 different languages. Global University, which came about as a merger of ICI University and Berean University, two missionary-related schools, offers video conferencing and internet-related curriculum as well as traditional print learning formats. Its motto is 'taking all the Word to all the World', stressing essential missionary and missionary-training objectives. Global University regards digital learning as crucial to its grass-roots approach which it calls the 'indigenous principle'. By the indigenous principle it means 'teaching believers overseas to reach their own people'.[74] Significant uses of distance learning have also been adopted in the missions training programme by such well-known entities as The School of World Missions at Fuller Theological Seminary, the Moody Bible Institute, Columbia Evangelical Seminary, and Bethany Bible College and Seminary.

The 'creative destruction' of the higher learning

'Globalization' in the digital sense will inevitably bring about the creative destruction of traditional higher education as global capitalism, following the predictions of Schumpeter, has done for economic institutions. Traditional higher education is distinguished by local monopolies, or regional oligopolies, over the knowledge process resulting from what might be described as the 'town and gown' syndrome. Institutions of the higher learning are economically, culturally, and historically integrated with a particular geographical locale, or topography. As advanced education has become more and more 'cosmopolitan' in scope, the pretensions of global learning have mushroomed. But what passes for 'global education' still amounts to the standard curricula of individual schools projected into exotic instructional settings, or some sort of odd pastiche of cross-cultural themes stitched together into a group of courses. If today's 'university' is ever to conform to the very etymology of the word (i.e. a 'unity' within diversity), then the knowledge space within which the faculty and students operate must expand exponentially beyond the conventional precincts of influence and control. At the same time, the sense of what the university actually is must transcend the history, traditions, constituencies, and social and national identities of particular schools, or clusters of schools.

In many ways this goal remains quite distant. Not only do the agendas as well as commercial and political strategies of particular institutions continue to override 'universal' thinking about higher education, but the development of the information architecture for a genuine 'global university' is still lacking. When the internet first began attracting attention and excitement in the mid-1990s, many utopians and futurists expected the rapid development of a vast 'information highway' network connecting and criss-crossing all sectors of the planet. In the first decade of the life of the internet the formal structure for that growth was put in place, as spider webs of fibre optic lines and other 'broadband pipes' were laid all the way from the cities of America's heartland to Australia to the endless and empty stretches of central Asia. But the 'content' that began to pass through those channels did not match up to the anticipation. The pornographic material and hate sites that proliferated in the early years of the internet were but one sign that Gresham's law – the rule that in a system of economic exchange the bad always drives out the good – applied not just to monetary policy, but also to digital culture. One of the main reasons obnoxious content began to dominate was the void left by the refusal of the vast majority of commercial publishers to enter the new virtual world of 'free' information.

Since the internet was originally designed to lower significantly, if not eliminate, the costs – and by inference the profits – of information delivery, this default was always understandable. However, it also had the perverse effect of sabotaging for the time being the entire 'new economy'. The bubble that was the new economy burst in the spring of 2000 not simply because of inflated price-to-earning ratios in stock, or what are now seen in retrospect as accounting machinations, but because of a fundamental instability at its very core. That instability derived from a fundamental contradiction that lurked at the heart of the new economy from the get-go. While the expansion of the new economy was always built on rising stock values justified by the expectation of higher future earnings from the digitization of both commerce and private life, the very process of digitization was aimed at countering the very dynamic of earnings, or return on capital. The economy of the late 1990s in many ways did not even measure up to being the classic 'Ponzi scheme' it has sometimes been called. Ponzi schemes at least are built to enrich early entrants who always get their money by the mathematical laws of compound accumulation. The new economy reached a point where even the first investors, if they hung on to their holdings, were burned, because the downward momentum of contraction turned out to be just as, if not more, merciless than the upward lift of equities speculation. The end result, which will affect the world economy over a very long haul, is that the global shift from finance capital to knowledge assets as the source of 'wealth' means that higher education will gradually shed its role as the dependent stepchild of the industrial economy. In the 'post-industrial' venue it will become the 'new industry'. The economic base, as many have predicted rhetorically, will become the new knowledge base. But this transformation will shake the foundations of the higher learning as brutally as it has begun to shake global capitalism itself.

The transition from financial to knowledge capital does not accord with the stereotypical political and economic views of either those on the left or on the right. Those on the left have hoped for years that the mounting economic importance of the higher learning would mean increased financial subsidies and support, particularly from national governments. Those on the right have looked toward the eventual replacement of state-directed institutions of post-secondary education with a proprietary or for-profit instructional industry that is not answerable to bureaucratic governing boards and ministries of education. They have yearned for the day when advanced learning would become a consumer durable that might be merchandised and sold in the global marketplace just like computer chips, fast food, automobiles, or cosmetics. Both dreams are not only antiquated, they are short-sighted. The 'creative' destruction of the world economy wrought by digital technology will bring in its wake the eventual collapse of the forms of mega-organization peculiar to the industrial age. Both right and left are wedded in their own fashion to corporatism and the corporate styles of 'command economies' that industrial production required. Corporatism, however, has always been antithetical to the free trafficking of information and the ethos of individual empowerment that the new knowledge age entails.

Digital technology offers a transparency to these structures, exposing them to the democratic daylight. The transactive nature of digital society means that the mass mobilization of resources characteristic of the old economy can only barely be sustained any longer. While these attempts at mobilization may foment the illusion of power and wealth for a brief interval, as happened during the stock market binge of the Nineties, the entire arrangement is destined to implode. 'Sustainability' is the watchword for the next era, though this term does not have the eco-political and romantic agrarian overtones it has assumed in the past generation. It refers to the sustainability of modest-scale modes of economic organization that are networked at different levels along with the technology itself. What strings together these different modes is the thread of transactivity that constantly shapes and replenishes the common knowledge base of the many cultures and societies. It is this thread that constitutes in a genuine fashion the 'global university'.

Open courseware

Another force that is beginning to sketch the shape for a global university is the innovation known as 'open courseware'. Pioneered at Massachusetts Institute of Technology (MIT), the open courseware concept was originally intended to disseminate course materials to students online, regardless of whether they were actually signed up for classes. MIT has undertaken to post the materials for about 2000 courses on the internet. According to *Syllabus* magazine, sceptics complained that open courseware 'would be nothing more than a traditional Web site dressed up with a new acronym'.[75] But proponents at MIT insist that the implications of the initiative are far more momentous.

The author of the article points out that in the salad days of the new economy colleges and universities sought to cash in on the digital revolution by creating proprietary courseware that could in principle be copyrighted, sold and exchanged like any form of intellectual property. Institutions of higher education have also sought in recent years to lay financial claim to the creative output of its researchers and instructors by recategorizing the production of digital content as 'work for hire', which effectively eliminates the personal copyright protection traditionally accorded to authors, artists, and intellectuals. The trend has also had the perverse effect of 'privatizing' knowledge, or localizing it, which was never the aim of the internet at the outset. Open courseware reverses these sorts of undesirable processes, which were already proving their lack of viability in the realm of commerce anyway. Open courseware speeds the globalization of knowledge without succumbing to the kinds of market disequilibrium that has marked global capitalism itself in the information age. The availability of the courseware fosters 'exploration' to the degree that 'one can discover interesting and useful associations between and among elements within the OCW collection of course content'.[76] In a word, the strategy of open courseware broadens the modes of access to information, creating more fertile ground for the metamorphosis of data into knowledge.

Economic analysis is beginning to show that the short-term failure of the new economy has not been due to the dynamics of the technology and the failure of the end user. It ensued from an original mismatch between the momentum of the digital revolution and the protocols of the old economy, centred on maximizing rate of return in the short run. The digital revolution did not start as a 'gold rush', which it quickly became in the minds of countless investors, business executives, and politicians, particularly in the Western world. It began in the early years principally as an effort both to enable and to accelerate the global exchange of information with the aim of creating an entire new 'capital base' – i.e. knowledge capital – for new and more socially productive societies. That capital base is still growing, but it is not proceeding in accordance with the rules of classical economics. To the extent that individual universities – even state-run institutions – behave like entrepreneurial players seeking to shore up their own 'bottom lines' with 'profitable' curricular ventures, they will fail. For the furtherance of the global university, and by extension the next phase of the global economy, depends on the 'internetworking' of information flows and knowledge transforms that the privatization of learning impedes. The new 'knowledge economy' is a strange breed, because it combines the contradictory impulses of competition and collaboration. Over the last two centuries, Adam Smith has been proven correct in his insight that the pursuit of private gain drives economic advance.

But the same principle, if applied to the pursuit of knowledge, works in reverse. In a knowledge economy the consequences of making education purely proprietary can be catastrophic. Education is social capital, or infrastructure. And the expansion of infrastructure means the optimizing of collaborative enterprise rather than heightened competition. If concrete highways had private toll-booths every few miles, the drag on commerce would be unbearable. By the same token, for the information 'highway' to be gated and metered at every juncture is to thwart its overarching purpose. That, unfortunately, is the precise effect which academic publishers with their meagre and overpriced print runs of books and journals, private universities with their astronomical tuition and fee structures that militate against the sharing of curricular enhancements, and the idolatry of 'elite' education which cordons off from general use the growing knowledge base has wrought.

Significantly, however, the hypercompetitive trends in contemporary learning may prove to be self-annihilating. According to Jason Ohler, 'one of the most poignant aspects of the virtual learning revolution is that it has turned what has traditionally been a seller's market into a buyer's market'.[77] The options which digital education affords are phenomenal. This proliferation of choices, despite efforts on the part of educational accrediting agencies to restrict them, is enlarging almost daily. Despite the fears of traditionalists that digital learning contexts would weaken the rigorous character of the older-style pedagogy, the opposite impact has occurred. The online format has made it much easier, and less expensive, to bring the student into engagement with classical objects of literacy from museum displays to text selections to multimedia sequences. What has changed is the cultural venue and the kinds of social practice and organization that support learning transactions. The most important shift of course is what we might term the unframing of educational content. In the past what one learned was always dependent on the availability of scarce curricular media and personnel (e.g. specialized textbooks, high-powered professors, the amenities of 'student life'). The scarcity of content went hand in hand with professional privilege and authority. In short, knowledge was always 'framed' by the special status of those who managed it. Digital education serves to unframe content insofar as it configures the value of learning not in terms of who authors it, or how it is provided, but with respect to how it plays in the vaster ensemble of conservation and inquiry. In that respect the proceedings of an online chat group can have as much educational value as, if not more than, an instructor's lecture notes. The openness of serious intellectual conversation in a web-based discussion forum can be even more important than a typical seminar, where the professor does most of the talking. The quality of knowledge generated in the session does not depend on the positioning of the 'expert' so much as on the interactions of the participants, who are free to exercise their skills and competencies without a 'teacher' defining and mediating them. If an instructor is very knowledgeable or has the gift of communication, his or her aptitudes will dominate the session and forward the knowledge process. But it will not be because the teacher has any sort of 'divine right' to steer the curriculum, but because he or she has the true competitive advantage in the marketplace of ideas. 'Free enterprise', therefore, is the motive force in the interpersonal sphere, rather than at the corporate level, where walls and boundaries come crashing down.

The global university is both the natural and inevitable outgrowth of the digital revolution, where the disintermediation of knowledge ensues directly from the interconnectivity and convergence of multiple information processes. This trend of disintermediation forges what we might describe as a 'universal space' for knowledge which is no longer conditioned by contingencies of culture and place. In a curious respect the coming of the postmodern university batters strongly against the intellectual tendencies of the past half-century, which has preferred the profusion of social particularities to what the period of the Enlightenment termed 'general truths of reason'. This development seems slightly paradoxical, because postmodernity is usually identified in the popular mind with conceptual relativism. The university, of course, was always founded on the Enlightenment idea, and it may take the spread of information technology, which relativizes the institutions of higher learning themselves through the growth of intellectual transactivity, to bring the higher learning back to its original moorings.

Chapter 9

Knowledge space

> Cyberspace: A consensual hallucination experienced daily by billions of legitimate operators, in every nation.
>
> (William Gibson)

The space of the postmodern university is an unbounded knowledge space. Since the founding of the European university system in the high Middle Ages, the space of knowledge has always been delineated by the social hierarchies and governmental structures that overshadow the 'educational' apparatus. For example, the early modern university was for the most part clerical and subordinate to the politics of the new nation-states rising across Northern Europe. The 'comprehensive' university that originated in nineteenth-century Prussia was built to articulate and legitimate the cultural complexity of the German state, while at the same time rationalizing the means of learning and instruction to comport with the new system of industrial production. The German state university, which became the model for the American land grant institution, was both distinctively 'democratic' and inherently 'bureaucratic', as the new industrial polity itself would become.[78] The notion that knowledge was something that could be 'produced' supplanted the former, ecclesiastical idea of knowledge as a form of transcendent and authoritative truth that had to be handed down and mediated from one generation of scholars to the next.

In fine, the knowledge spaces of the past have always been ordered in accordance with a miscellany of political, social, economic, demographic, and geographic differences. The way in which we still think – nostalgically – of higher education to this day mirrors this time-tested model. Any 'Ivy League' school, no matter how comparable its curriculum to other prestige institutions, retains of necessity a certain historical, social, and conceptual identity that has little to do with the bare intellectual activity that transpires within its bailiwick.

Cyberspace as knowledge space

But the knowledge space of the new university increasingly is the space of what we know as 'cyberspace'. In at least the past decade the term 'cyberspace' has become a familiar item in our lexicon. More recently, the extent of cyberspace has been associated with the internet itself. However, the thought of cyberspace is both older and richer than the technological archetype of digital networks we have discussed so far. As Margaret Wertheim has pointed out, the conception of cyberspace constitutes in many ways a return to the Medieval understanding of a metaphysical distinction between physical and 'spiritual' or 'sacred' space. Like the peculiar 'space' of heaven and hell, which Medieval people considered contiguous with the physical universe and believed to be populated with spirits, angels, archangels and demons, cyberspace is an equally present, and equally 'real', realm where the order of things, not to mention the range of possibilities, is distinctly different from everyday phenomena. The 'new digital space', she remarks, 'is "beyond" the space that physics describes, for the cyber-realm is not made up of physical particles and forces, but of *bits* and *bytes*. These packets of data are the ontological foundation of cyberspace, the seeds from which the global phenomena emerges'.[79]

The expression 'cyberspace' was coined by science fiction writer William Gibson and first appears in his 'cyberpunk' novel, published in 1984 and entitled *Neuromancer*. In the early phases of its use it connoted a kind of electro-narcotic fantasy space. 'Cyberculture', as the early history of the internet itself suggests, was little more than an up-to-date, second-generation rendering of the Sixties counterculture.[80] It was a domain where computer simulations converged with, or substituted for, acid trips. Cyberspace was the realm of 'virtual reality', a cosmos in which anything imaginable was not only possible, but actual, where dream and myth coalesced with perception, where sensation and the simulation of sense remained indistinguishable. It even had a place name – what Rushkoff dubbed 'cyberia'.[81] Cyberspace, therefore, could be characterized as a kind of space where the conventional difference between the real and the unreal were essentially indiscernible, where the limitless connectivity of information was engrafted into the untrammelled power of the human imagination. As one of the 'cyberian' characters interviewed by Rushkoff declares: 'We don't want [cyberspace] to look like it takes place in a natural setting. We want it to all be self-contained in a conceptual space that's primarily videographic ... it'll be the reality of the imagination. We've quit trying to mimic reality; we try to mimic our imagination, which is the root of all reality anyway'.[82]

This notion of a 'reality' that is nevertheless 'unreal', or one that is 'more real than real', has been a staple of Baudrillard's social philosophy. In fact, in many circles Baudrillard is coming to be regarded as the postmodern philosopher par excellence. Such a reality is what Baudrillard terms 'hyperreality'. The hyperreal consists in a reality that is indistinguishable from illusion. 'The impossibility of rediscovering an absolute level of the real is of the same order as the impossibility of staging illusion. Illusion is no longer possible, because the real is no longer possible.'[83]

Like so many postmodernist constructs of philosophy, the hyperreal is more 'hyperbolic' than descriptive. In short, it is less a useful theory of how things are than a rhetorical challenge to rethink postmodern experience and knowledge. If reality is tending toward the hyperreal, then the 'lay' architecture of knowledge in the postmodern era must be progressively 'hypercognitive'. The hypercognitive, in turn, implies a knowledge space that is unrelated to physical space, and, as with hyperreality itself, involves a movement of 'simulacra' that are not traditionally associated with the usual 'divisions' of subject areas and curricula. What can we understand by a knowledge space that is independent of the physical space of classrooms, college buildings, and 'residential' campuses, or the instructional space of textbooks, term papers, and final exams? It is a space that media theorist Margaret Morse calls 'immersional'. Immersional space is total space. It 'transgresses' physical space to the degree that the sinews and ligatures of what we normally intuit as 'material existence' are airbrushed away, and there is no passable borderland between data, dreams, phantoms, and 'spiritual' entities. Morse writes that 'virtual worlds are the solely virtual or immaterial realms with which one interacts to varying degrees in varying modes of personhood. While virtual worlds can seek to reproduce natural landscapes, there is a thrill of transgression in entering a symbolic landscape or metaphor of what would other-wise be inaccessible and impenetrable'.[84] Participation in this virtual universe, according to Morse, is to enter a kind of dreamworld. She compares the process to an immersion in the symbolic syntax, 'in language itself', as though what postmodernists call the 'gram-matology', or system of material signification, were in itself an alter-native universe of sorts. It is truly a venture similar to Alice through the looking glass.

Immersional space

The knowledge space of the postmodern university is both immer-sional and open space. It is a true electronic frontier, a kind of intel-lectual commons that has not existed in the 'cloistered' or walled spatiality of the higher learning for at least a millennium. Para-doxically, as living space, particular in America, becomes more and more codified and constricted because of excessive development and carefully defined land use, learning space expands expo-nentially. Constraints on mobility in today's 'megapolitan' living settings – ever lengthening traffic tie-ups, limited mass transit – encourage the infinite mobility of computer-mediated communica-tion and the illimitable gyring of packet-switched information flows. The same paradox can be detected in the transformation of the university in general. As cities and suburbs become more 'medieval' with their gated condominium communities and high-rise office parks, the last institution of the Middle Ages, the univer-sity itself, lunges into the *terra incognita* of postmodernity. The walls of knowledge, like the Berlin Wall itself, collapse before post-industrial pressures for democratization.

As with all movements of historical change, however, the passage from old to new is shot through with indications and contradictions. One of the most critical questions facing chroniclers of the digital revolution is the degree in which knowledge can be dispersed and distributed without a focal, or 'authorial', dimension. A case can be made that the networking and proliferation of 'nodes' within the new universe of digital communications must simply create an amorphous flux of 'information' that has not completely coalesced into knowledge. Digital culture makes possible the broad augmenta-tion of new approaches to learning and the construction of alternate visions of the different academic 'disciplines'. But as yet there has been a significant refusal to draw lines and set boundaries, which is what any 'epistemological' standard, any general theory of knowledge, demands.

Online education, or 'e-learning' as it is now starting to be called, involves much more than the interaction of students and professors through email, or the dissemination of lectures via web pages. It entails a wholly unprecedented synthesis of intellect, imagination, and technical competency. There is a decided difference between listening to a Mahler symphony on a CD player with headphones and playing a violin in the very orchestra performing the piece. In a profound sense the online education experience is akin to stroking the violin. One's own role in the performance is not unrelated to the outcome. Specifically, one's personal competence or participation helps define the 'structures' of knowledge that emerge. A symphony, of course, is played in accordance with a prior score. But there is no script for the way in which knowledge is consolidated in the postmodern university setting. The open architecture of digital instruction raises the most fundamental question of what we mean by knowledge at all, and how such things as 'curricular', or 'degree, requirements' as well as fields of inquiry can be envisaged within the new archetype.

Whereas the promise and prospects of cyberexperience may have been advanced in the early years of the technology revolution by designer drug-ingesting techies in warehouse offices of San Francisco's South Bay, who were role-playing for the early Nineties the entrenched myths of Bohemia in the Sixties, such a world is now long gone, having passed over into the workaholic and finance-driven frenzy of the 'dot.com' culture. So far as the university itself is concerned, the impetus for educational change has not come from the psychedelic dens of dorm rooms but from corporate interests who have been pushing digital learning as a way of forcing autonomous academics to accede to their very pragmatic and bottom-line agenda.[85] But the free-form and libertarian ethos of the early cyber-revolution cannot be domesticated. And its spirit cannot be broken by either the demands of the corporate 'organization man' or the attempt to colonize cyberculture with the accoutrements of traditional academics. The new learning values that surfaced with the individualistic trends of the Sixties and Seventies, for better or worse, have been reinforced by the momentum of the technological tide itself.

The case of the University of Oklahoma

Curiously, however, the postmodern university in America seems to be emerging in a place known neither for its West Coast cultural trendiness nor its concentration of high tech startup firms. Norman, Oklahoma, where the University of Oklahoma is located, is a cameo of a vanishing, small-town, middle American culture. It is a different sort of 'OU' than Britain's Open University, but the outcomes are very similar. Higher education system in Oklahoma was from its beginnings a 'distributed' system of learning.

This historical peculiarity arose from the unique genealogy of the state of Oklahoma itself. Before 1889, Oklahoma was known as 'Indian Territory' – a huge swatch of land that the federal government in its forced removal of tribes from the Southeast during the administration of Andrew Jackson deeded to various Indian nations. For over a century now Indians, Anglos, African-Americans, and recent immigrant groups have lived together in Oklahoma as a multi-ethnic state within the United States. But the tribal demographics of the state tended to de-centralize the administration of higher learning. Most of Oklahoma's small, regional universities started out as tribal schools. In addition, the thoroughly rural character of Oklahoma meant that 'correspondence courses', as distance education before the advent of computers and telecommunications was called, were the rule rather than the exception. Oklahoma leaped into distance learning at the statewide level long before it became fashionable in American higher education. Oklahoma State University in Stillwater early on became known as one of the national pace-setters in distance delivery of courses. Such a culture of distributed instruction has promoted the rapid growth of internet-based learning.

Until one comes upon the university itself with its steel and glass towers, low-rise classroom buildings, and campus greenbelt, one acquires the feeling quickly that they have journeyed back in time to a more nostalgic era. But OU, known nationally on the main for its top-ten football teams, is pushing full-steam into the digital sunrise faster than any post-secondary institution of its ilk or size. The action, however, is not on the regular campus, but in a special unit known as the College of Liberal Studies.

The College of Liberal Studies was at one time a predominantly 'correspondence' school. This type of institution, viewed condescendingly for decades by older, more prestigious schools, was the natural matrix for the evolution of postmodern learning spaces. The College of Liberal Studies has developed its internet program on top of its existing interdisciplinary program called the Bachelor of Liberal Studies/Classic. There are no routine course 'distribution' requirements or discipline-based courses in the degree format, even though the college follows both university and state general education requirements. Instructors have regular appointments to the University of Oklahoma faculty. The curriculum combines independent study, involving readings, writing, and research projects, with short-term, on-campus seminars of an intensive nature. The degree is 'self-paced', which means that students are allowed to undertake and finish assignments on their own terms and within a flexible time frame. Independent studies last for one year.

The freshman and sophomore years consist of a 2-credit introductory seminar scheduled for the start of every fall and spring semester. The seminar is held for two consecutive weekends. It is followed by 12-credit modules in the humanities, natural sciences, and social science as well as by two 12-hour 'area' seminars in the winter and spring. The junior and senior years consist of three 8-hour blocks of interdisciplinary study, again in the humanities, natural sciences, and social sciences; a 12-credit area seminar; a 12-hour 'inter-area study'; an inter-area seminar; and a concluding block of 'study in depth' for 4 hours.

According to the brochure, the Bachelor of Liberal Studies 'was one of the first degree programs in the United States designed specifically for adult, part-time students'.[86] In 1967 the college added a master's program. Three years later liberal studies was transformed from a 'program' into an independent college as part of the Oklahoma system. It currently has its own dean and administrative structure.

> The College of Liberal Studies views the Internet as a powerful new teaching and learning tool. The BLS/GIS was created as a curricular alternative to the BLS/Classic program for those students seeking a flexible, yet more structured, way to complete their degree. Unlike the open-ended enrollments of the BLS/Classic, enrollments in the BLS/GSIS are completed within a fall or spring semester timeframe.[87]

Curricular materials are all supplied through the internet. Reading and writing assignments involve online research. All assignments, as is characteristic of most digital learning, are conducted through email.

Enrolment in the BLS/IGIS demands what the brochure calls a 'working knowledge of personal computers'. This requirement is not as earth-shaking as it could have been earlier in the digital revolution, but it is still an admissions line that most colleges and universities, not willing to turn away certain students, refuse to draw in the sand. At the same time, admission standards for the college are the same as other units of the university, and the growth of BLS programs confirms the popularity of the digital archetype.

The prime movers in the development of the BLS/IGIS are Robert J. Dougherty, MLS, Coordinator for Departmental Computing Systems for the College of Liberal Studies, and Susan Smith Nash, Ph.D., Director of Engineering and Geosciences for the College of Continuing Education. Dougherty's background is in computer sciences. Nash has a doctorate in English and is herself a specialist in postmodernist theory. They are co-authors of the book *The Diamond Solution: Keys to Successful Online Course Development and Administration*, and have talked about their experience with the development of computer-based liberal arts programs at various national meetings. I myself came to know them at the annual *Syllabus* conference, the leading national gathering of online curricular planners and developers, in Silicon Valley during the summer of 1999.

In their book Dougherty and Nash offer a no-holds-barred, down-to-earth analysis of what is possible, and what is not so possible, with online instruction. They dispel at the outset many of the fantasies and unrealistic expectations both educational reformers, and digital hucksters share concerning the promise of a wired academy. They caution against entrancement by the apparent 'magic of the internet' and demand that course designers take careful inventory of the myriad hardware and software problems both students and faculty can experience in elaborating strategies for delivery. They also talk about the headaches associated with internet service providers and access problems associated with rural phone lines.

But the key contribution of the authors to the burgeoning discussions of online learning is what they call 'the Diamond Solution'. *The Diamond Solution* is founded on an equable integration of what the authors consider the four indispensible roles in electronic education – those of faculty, student, curriculum web site developer, and network manager. Many institutions attempt, according to the authors, to build online instructional platforms by seriously employing only one or two of these particular 'players'. Quite commonly faculty are turned loose on their own to come up with something that will appeal to students, whose opinions are not even consulted. The success of online learning is only possible, however, when both teachers and techies are taking part as a single, dedicated design unit. All four functions have to be constantly engaged, and conversant with, each other for the online venture to achieve its optimal goals. The authors warn, in particular, against loading the faculty member with the responsibilities of a technical administrator. 'Their role in being the flag-bearers of the subject matter and their academic interaction with the student is what makes for the best learning/teaching environment.'[88]

The job of technical administrator should be handled by the network manager. He, or she, should not be assigned to curricular tasks, or to academic development of any kind. His or her expertise is, and should be, simply technological. Finally, the instructor should have the appreciable benefit of a curricular site architect. The web site developer should understand pedagogical principles and how they are applied to a digital environment. But they should not be concerned with content, which the faculty member oversees.

Nash, in particular, has developed this instructional blueprint from the application of postmodernist literary theory on which she did her doctoral dissertation. She first took an interest in online courses working on her dissertation, which involved a study of apocalyptic narrative in film, literature, and the culture at large and the way it encouraged people to join end-of-the-world cults or to gravitate toward extremism. The internet itself interested Nash because of its immense diversity of content and cultural expression. 'I was able to see', she says, 'how the semiotic functioned within a persuasive context. So, I thought it would be helpful for students if they had a supplementary web site for the classes I happened to be teaching – one which would link to thought-provoking sites, and which would encourage them to make connections between the material and their own lives.'[89] The transition from using the internet as a curricular supplement to developing an entire web-oriented programme 'with an underlying philosophy of internet-generated epistemologies' came about gradually.

The multi-nodal distribution of learning applications, as outlined in the diamond theory, derives from the postmodernist notion of the mobile signifier. In postmodernist conceptions of meaning there is no central 'content' that determines what something 'stands for'. Meaning is established both by context and the 'trespass' of one sign upon the territory of the other. Meaning is a function of differentiation within a signifying web. In the same vein the 'diamond solution' constitutes a matrix of differentiated learning practices which overcome the traditional duality of the teacher and the taught, the learner and the one who dispenses or discharges 'learning'. In philosophical terms we are talking about the erasure of the familiar subject–object dichotomy. In its stead we have the nonlocality and geographical contingency of the signifying moment.

Pedagogically speaking, we are talking about the 'errancy' of the learning act itself. Nash puts it this way:

> Online learning further problematizes subjectivity by detaching logos from its accoutrement of hierarchically-determined (and enforced) signification; it places the newly unleashed *logos* in the hands of the empowered websurfer who can appropriate the ['content' of the message] by a re-reification of logos and meaning.

A case in point, she argues, is the student who cuts and pastes images as well as sundry texts without attribution in an assignment that is then uploaded onto a webserver. The *logos*, or form of knowledge, is not 'sited' in accordance with its authoritative 'document' sources. The *logos* is free-ranging; it wanders and multiplies. Furthermore, the 'subjectivity' of the learner is no longer an issue. 'Subjectivity is subsumed into what becomes a decentred discourse of resistance – one that resists the re-formation of the pseudo-essentialism . . . the logos-heavy consumer culture of Western societies.'[90]

Nash goes on to make this point in a less recondite manner. In the regular classroom, she says, information is always 'sequenced'. 'The logic structure lends itself to causal structures, and certain if-then arrangements of conclusions. This is probably inescapable, given the structure of in-class presentations, and it is one reason logical fallacies are so insidious and difficult to eradicate.' One of the most pervasive fallacies is the idea that a traditional classroom can have 'spontaneous' discussions. Traditional classrooms allow conversations about as spontaneous as they are in a court of law where one is sitting before a judge and jury. In the traditional classroom the teacher acts not so much as a judge as the theatre director in the shadows. The instructor sets the stage, directs the performers, and preps the audience. He or she functions as a 'logic cop'. The reality of traditional education gives the lie to the oft-recited platitude among liberal learning advocates that the classroom is a 'laboratory' for real life. The traditional classroom is more like a 'finishing school' for those who have been pre-selected for the process in the first place.[91]

The internet 'changes all this', Nash notes. Although the internet in recent years has taken on many of the characteristics of 'logo-centric' mass media, it retains the potential to distribute perceptions of significance in a broad and non-hierarchical fashion. Nash cites the example of standard, avante-garde artistic techniques, which work very well in online courses. In the 1960s these techniques were known as 'happenings', consisting of impromptu forms of staged expression and random locations. Artists would do 'crazy' things like glue spaghetti on road signs. In art theory the happening erased distinction between the context and frame of the artwork. Art learned to 'unframe' its content long before education. Standard assumptions about the point and purpose of 'portraiture, art-production, and sculpture' all went out the window with 'the happening'.[92]

It is quite possible, Nash observes, to do the same with online content design. One can create a 'malleable' web site where students can fill out a form and substitute graphics and words for their own. An instructor can encourage deliberate tampering with the web site to get the point across that the electronic text is now 'decentred' and bereft of its authority, in the same way that avant-garde art has sought to remove the overweening presence of the artists. An analogy is the work of artist Barbara Kruger, who in the 1980s and 1990s created her own billboards. These new billboards were 'based on (and ultimately subversive of) normal billboards, and they focused on the commercialization of art, consumer culture, and consumer mentalities vis-à-vis art'.[93] New web-based information can concomitantly be both based on, and transgressive toward, the web as a communications medium. In this, 'subversion' of the communications medium, and the educational horizons that opens up, becomes the task itself. This task is commissioned by the fact that the new knowledge space is anti-hierarchical and anti-'subjective'. It is no longer the case that, as Marshall McLuhan long ago proclaimed, 'the medium is the message'. The message and the medium are now obverse, or complementary, facets of each other. The 'message' arises from the dispersion of the medium, which is radically anti-aristocratic. The event of meaning/learning is now a 'happening' that depends on the confluence of both strategic and aesthetic practices. Like the arts themselves, learning moves into the 'streets'.

Knowledge space and the information grid

The difference between knowledge under the older instructional regimes and knowledge today, on the other hand, is that such knowledge is now embedded within what internet entrepreneur Jay Walker terms the 'information grid'. The current revolution in business habits and processes can be explained, according to Walker, by the social dominance of this grid. Before the internet other grids such as highways, electricity, and communications systems were in the ascendancy.

But the reticular spread of information is now more important than these familiar systems. The information grid, says Walker, soon 'will subsume many of the functions of the other grids'. In a very important respect the new knowledge matrix can be described as 'the Grid of Grids'. The grid in information theory is comparable to the cerebral cortex, as understood in biology. It is the cellular mass that makes us different from the rest of the animal world. According to Walker, the cerebral cortex is 'the seat of our higher reasoning powers'. It makes possible our facility for memory and the cognitive functions that depend on memorization. 'Because of the Internet, we are living in the age of the wiring of the cerebral cortex of all of society.'[94]

It is ironic, if not dangerous in various serious ways to society as a whole, that so much of higher education refuses to join the grid. Can one imagine a major city in the late twentieth century refusing to be tied into the national power grid, or the grid of interstate highways? It is entirely unimaginable. If such were the case, the threat to the national economy, if not national security, would be extraordinary. But that is exactly what is happening with higher education. Despite its enormous price tag, it is adamantly resisting efforts to connect it with the ubiquitous information grid that is permeating the culture at large.

A study of the rate of adoption of so-called 'distance learning' strategies by political science departments in America – a bell-weather faculty for the liberal arts and general education – is truly alarming. It is not our contention that the implementation of regular distance delivery models on a broad scale constitutes any significant measure of true technological innovation in the classroom. But the study revealed the deep, almost phobic reaction of faculty to all technological redescriptions of learning space. The authors of the study gloomily conclude that 'the level of interest in distance learning demonstrated by the chairs of political science departments was low overall'. Indeed the average degree of knowledge was also pitifully inferior. 'These data are important', the authors surmise, 'because they indicate that if future growth is likely to occur in distance learning in the field of political science, it is unlikely to come from institutions and faculty as educators.'[95]

Institutional resistance to technological transformation may not, however, be primarily a matter of crypto-Ludditism. It may have more to do with the way in which higher education has found itself boxed in by the sputtering industrial economy and the tacit industrial model of organization that still suffuses post-secondary instruction. As Stephen Talbott argues, the real 'threat' to higher education does not arise directly from any likelihood that genuine teaching functions can be successfully automated, as so many faculty fear. It has more to do with the fact that the higher educational system has already been so dumbed down and routinized that any kind of technological surrogation will not make much difference anyway. Talbott stresses that the now normative view in American society, and in the administration of learning, that knowledge is nothing but 'the transfer of information from one database or brain to another' has made the fantasy of a pure, professorless production facility for 'knowledge' plausible in the first place. So much of distance education in fact is an effort to implement such a model. Yet this model was bankrupt long before technology took over. 'What we haven't realized', says Talbott, 'is that this fact-shovelling model of education renders both teachers and schools superfluous. It's true that many colleges and universities have struggled mightily to convert themselves into more efficient vehicles for information delivery. But they can hardly hope to compete successfully with the computer in this sterile game.'[96]

The false promise of 'corporate education'

In other words, computers and standard 'distance delivery' versions of education just might, in fact, do what so much of the professoriate fears if our vision of what education itself means does not change. The industrial model of higher education is still tempting, particularly to corporate America. However, as Talbott ironically makes us recognize, it is itself ridiculously costly and inefficient, inasmuch as it fails to mobilize and optimize the power of the new information technology as a handmaiden to learning in the richer sense of the word. Just as the corporate television moguls discovered after millions of wasted investment dollars that they could not duplicate the older forms of cable, or broadcast media on the internet, so the same captains of industry will quickly ascertain, if they have not done so already, that standardized 'knowledge manufacturing' installations (read 'universities') will no longer suffice in the digital climate.

It has often been said that one's friends are potentially their worst enemies. Contrary to corporate techie mythology, the ideal of a Microsoft or Intel U where students learn through streamlined 'courseware' modules, and traditional types of knowledge specialization are transmogrified into business applications, can never be viable. The reason is not that opaque. The knowledge space of networked digital communications is a vastly different space than what has characterized historically the methods of industrial production. The knowledge space of the industrial university is top-down and command-centred. The knowledge space of the post-industrial, or postmodern university, parallels that of the world wide web itself. It is topologically defracted as well as 'de-centred', which is to say it is *client-controlled*. The explosion of distributed computing at the social and economic level can only mean the radical distribution of both knowledge production and consumption within the emerging 'telecosm'.

In a more recent interview, Perelman has attempted to go beyond the quasi-utopian reveries of *School's Out* to prophesy the imminent collapse of the American educational system because of many of the same factors that led Communism to fall apart in the late 1980s. As with Communism, Perlman insists, the debacle must ultimately be economic. And the 'new economy' is by its very logic and dynamic inimical to 'traditional learning'. Perelman enlarges upon his original construct of 'hyperlearning' as a pedagogical effect of networked computing environments to describe it as a way 'to put a label on the web of postacademic knowledge processes that is the driving force of the new economy'.[97] Perelman's fundamental argument, as it evolved during the 1990s, was that 'the end of education' does not signify its extinction so much as its increasing irrelevance to the formation and acquisition of knowledge in today's culture. If it were not for the degree-credentialing system and the school accrediting system that is universally run by and for the educational bureaucracy, education would have succumbed much more rapidly to the worldwide forces of market restructuring. Education cannot be 'reformed', Perelman emphasizes, because education is the problem itself. Education is in effect a 'command economy' for the generation of knowledge. And command economies invariably fail to deliver the goods.

Many corporate executives, including probably many disciples of Perelman, however, have failed to grasp that the substitution of one form of command (the educational) for another (the corporate/ industrial) is no solution. The business model of education, when all has been said and done, is still business-as-usual. The recent crisis of the 'new economy' has made that clear. Lenin once defined Communism as 'soviets plus electrification'. It took fifty years to realize that the problem with Communism was the soviets, not the latter. Similarly, the problem with corporate education is that it is 'corporate' to begin with. Right now corporate education is experiencing the same crisis as the soviet model of industrial economy did in the 1980s.

Hyperlearning, and by extension the hyperuniversity, entails a culture of intellectual freedom like the familiar academy. But it is a freedom borne not of the neo-aristocratic systems of tenure and privilege that are a vanishing institution even in 'traditional higher education', but of the dynamism of a globally extensive, open architecture of client-driven questing and transactivity. The 'net' is the bet for the next generation of 'formal' learning, not merely because it is the worldwide information packaging system of choice, but because it is swiftly redefining the channels through which all information on its way to becoming knowledge must flow. As the dot.com phenomenon, despite its momentary economic shortfalls, has shown, the information economy requires a whole new kind of institutional space that pervades both workplace and 'schoolyard'. This new institutional space reconfigures the entirety of social knowledge space.

Perelman may very well be correct when he foretells the economic collapse of traditional education. But the collapse – hopefully it will be a crisis that can be eventually resolved – will not come simply as a result of commercial educational 'providers' doing a better job of the same old same old, as certain educational reform pundits have predicted for more than a decade now. It will because the very archetype of social and intellectual organization that has subsisted in our minds for centuries crumbles as well.

Many of us are still Medievalists when it comes to 'learning'. Instead we need to learn to become postmodernists bent on the great intellectual adventure which, even with all our cant about the 'life of the mind', we have refused to undertake. In the history of education the 'life of the mind' has always been coded and framed to give us a certain sort of privileged signification. Though we speak of 'knowledge', the referent is always the brick and mortar that houses the clanking, 'authorized' apparatus for its production. That is why we become confused these days when we speak of the 'university'. The confusion results when we, as former serfs labouring on behalf of the lord of the manor, realize that the castle is now weather-beaten, inconsequential, and empty.

Just as Wittgenstein has shown us that the university is not the buildings, so we must discern a filament of metaphor in the study by French philosopher Michel Foucault of the work of the great surrealist painter René Magritte. One of Magritte's most famous paintings is entitled *Ceci n'est pas une pipe* – 'This is Not a Pipe'. The painting juxtaposes the 'picture' of the pipe with its verbal caption and asks us to identify the 'object'. As Foucault points out, 'it is quite apparent that the drawing representing the pipe is not the pipe itself'.[98] But as Magritte makes us realize, the 'pipe itself' is located neither in the 'thing' that appears to be 'represented' nor in the verbal description. The pipe can only be found in the exploding network of significations, conundra, and interpolations that enable us to somehow decipher this puzzle. By the same token, the postmodern university must be glimpsed in the efflorescent complexity of threads, links, sites, simulations, protocols, logics, and connections that somehow earn the name of 'the net'. There may be local and intense activity within certain physical spaces that are part of this net, and we will call them particular 'institutions'. But they are not the 'university'. There is an old joke among physicists about the professor who walked into his classroom and posed the following question to his students: 'define the universe, and give three examples'. The punch line, of course, is that the universe by definition cannot be parlayed into 'examples'. It is simply the unity of everything that can be distinguished or diversified. As knowledge permutates and diversifies in the same manner, we are tempted to give 'examples' of the 'university'. But it can only be 'one'. It is the space of all knowledge spaces.

Notes

1　Luther A. Weigle, *American Idealism* (new Haven: Yale University Press, 1928), p. 304.
2　Hans Bertens, *The Idea of the Postmodern: A History* (London and New York: Routledge, 1995), p. 5.
3　Baudrillard writes: 'Today consumption . . . defines precisely the stage where the commodity is immediately produced as a sign, as sign value, and where signs (culture) are produced as commodities.' See Jean Baudrillard, 'The Political Economy of the Sign', in Mark Poster (ed.), *Jean Baudrillard: Selected Writings* (Stanford CA: Stanford University Press, 1988), p. 80.
4　Quoted in *InfoWorld Electric* (November 16, 1999).
5　Pierre Lévy, *Collective Intelligence* (Cambridge MA: Perseus Books, 1997), p. 3.
6　See E.A. Burtt, *Metaphysical Foundations of Modern Science* (New York: Prometheus Books, 1999).
7　Gilles Deleuze and Felix Guittari, *A Thousand Plateaus* (Minneapolis: University of Minnesota Press, 1987).
8　Deleuze and Guittari, p. 25.
9　Steven Best and Douglas Kellner, *Postmodern Theory: Critical Interrogations* (New York: The Guilford Press, 1991), p. 99.
10　Consider Werner Kelber's thesis that 'modes of communication were themselves potential embodiments of cognition and shapers of consciousness'. See his '1994 Lord and Parry Lecture', *Oral Tradition* (1995): 411–450.
11　Charles Jencks, 'What is Postmodernism?' in Lawrence E. Cahoone, *From Modernism to Postmodernism: An Anthology* (London: Blackwell, 1996).Lewis J. Perelman, *School's Out: Hyperlearning, the New Technology, and the End of Education* (New York: William Morrow and Company, Inc., 1992), p. 7.
12　Lewis J. Perelman, *School's Out: Hyperlearning, the New Technology, and the End of Education* (New York: William Morrow and Company, Inc., 1992), p. 7.
13　Perelman, p. 22.
14　Perelman, p. 28.

15 Peter J. Denning, 'Business Designs for the New University', *Educom Review* Vol. 31, No. 6 (November/December 1996), http://www.educause.edu/pub/er/review/reviewArticles/31620.html.

16 Educom Review Staff, 'A Matter of Degrees: Colorado Governor Roy Romer on the Western Governors University', *Educom Review*, Vol. 32, No. 1 (January/February 1997), http://www.educause.edu/pub/er/review/reviewArticles/32116.html.

17 'The Future of Learning: An Interview with Alfred Bork', *Educom Review* (July/August 1999), http://www.educause.edu/ir/library/html/erm9946.html.

18 See, among others, Eli Noam, 'The End of the University', *Science*, October 13, 1995; Educom Review Staff, 'Eli Noam on the Future of the University', *Educom Review*, Vol. 31, No. 4 (July/August 1996), http://www.educause.edu/pub/er/review/reviewArticles/31438.html; Educom Staff, 'Talking with George Gilder', Vol. 29, No. 4 (July/August 1994), http://www.educause.edu/pub/er/review/reviewArticles/29432.html; Peter Drucker, *Forbes* (March 10, 1997).

19 Louis Menand, 'Everybody Else's College Education', *New York Times Magazine*.

20 William F. Massy and Robert Zemsky, 'Using Information Technology to Enhance Academic Productivity', *Educause* Archives, http://www.educause.edu/nlii/keydocs/massy.html.

21 Robert C. Heterick, Jr, and John Gehl, 'Information Technology and the Year 2000', *Educom Review*, Vol. 30, No. 1 (January/February 1995), http://www.educause.edu/pub/er/review/reviewArticles/30122.html.

22 See among other research J.R. Anderson, A.T. Corbett, K.R. Koedinger, and R. Pelletier, 'Cognitive Tutors: Lessons Learned, *Journal of the Learning Sciences*, Vol. 4, 167–208; J.V. Boettcher, *101 Success Stories of Information Technology in Higher Education: The Joe Wyatt Challenge* (New York: McGraw-Hill, 1993); G.V. Blass, B. McGraw, and M.L. Smith, *Meta-Analysis in Research* (Beverly Hills CA: Sage Publications, 1981); M.J. Hannafin, K.M. Hannafin, S.R. Hooper, L.P. Rieber, and A.S. Kini, 'Research On, and Research With, Emerging Technologies', in D.H. Jonassen (ed.), *Handbook of Research for Educational Communications and Technology* (New York: Simon and Schuster, 1996), pp. 378–402.

23 Neal H. Brodsky, 'Learning from Learners, Internet-Style', *Educom Review*, Vol. 33, No. 2 (March/April 1998), http://www.educause.edu/pub/er/review/reviewArticles/33214.html.

24 An interesting book that explores the 'mind' of the net-proficient younger generation, though somewhat dated and overhyped, is Douglas Rushkoff, *Playing the Future: What We Can Learn from Digital Kids* (New York: Riverhead Books, 1999). A popular write and oracle of today's culture of cyberhip, Rushkoff argues that a kind of generational mutation may have taken place.

25 Some major resources on active learning as applied to online pedagogy include H. Schweizer, *Designing and Teaching an Online Course: Spinning Your Web Classroom* (Needham Heights MA: Allyn & Bacon, 1999); W.J. Gibbs, 'Implementing On-line Learning Environments",

Journal of Computing in Higher Education, Vol. 10, No. 1 (Fall 1998), pp. 16–37; Carol Guardo and Scott Rivinius, 'Save Before Closing: Bringing Technology to the Liberal Arts', *Liberal Education*, Vol. 81 (Summer 1995), pp. 22–27.

26 Warren Baker, Thomas Hale, and Bernard R. Gifford, 'From Theory to Implementation: The Mediated Learning Approach to Computer-Mediated Instruction, Learning and Assessment', *Educom Review*, Vol. 32, No. 5 (September/October 1997), http://www.educause.edu/pub/er/review/reviewArticles/32542.html

27 Mark C. Taylor, *Hiding* (Chicago: University of Chicago Press, 1997), p. 325.

28 Hegel's most important work, where the notion of dialectic is developed, is his *Phenomenology of Spirit*, trans. A.V. Miller (New York: Oxford University Press, 1979). See also his *Philosophy of History* (New York: Dover Publications, 1956).

29 Quoted in Otis Port, 'The Next Web', *Business Week* (March 4, 2002), p. 98.

30 Chester E. Finn and Theodor Rebarber, *Education Reform in the 90s* (New York: Macmillan, 1992), p. xv.

31 See George M. Marsden, *The Soul of the American University: From Protestant Establishment to Established Nonbelief* (New York: Oxford University Press, 1994).

32 'It's time to start talking less about information infrastructure and more about information metastructure: less about protocols and more about purpose: less about the where and when of education (breaking down walls of time and space) and more about the what and why of education (breaking down walls of bureaucracy so that individuals are treated as individuals rather than as cattle)', John Gehl, 'The Curriculum Has Run its Course', *Educom Review*, Vol. 31 (November/December 1996),

33 Athansios Moulakis, *Beyond Utility: Liberal Education for a Technological Age* (Columbia MO: University of Missouri Press, 1994), p. 133.

34 Barbara M. Stafford, 'Educating Digerati', *Arts Education Policy Review*, Vol. 99, 1998.

35 A good, practical article on how this process works is Robert Vojtek and Roseanne O'Brien Vojtek, 'How to Guide Students Through the Banquet of the Web', *Journal of Staff Development*, Vol. 19, 1998.

36 Robert and Jon Solomon, *Up the University: Re-Creating Higher Education in America* (Reading MA: Addison-Wesley Publishing Company, 1993), p. 225.

37 Kenneth E. Hay, 'Legitimate Peripheral Participation, Instructionism, and Constructivism: Whose Situation Is It Anyway', in Hilary McLellan (ed.), *Situated Learning Perspectives* (Englewood Cliffs NJ: Educational Technology Publications, 1996), p. 91.

38 Stephen J. Bostock, 'Constructivism in Mass Education: A Case Study', *British Journal of Educational Technology* Vol. 29, 1998. For some key pieces of literature on collaborative learning, see M.W. Caprio (ed.), *From Traditional Approaches Toward Innovation* (The Society for

College Science Teachers: The SCST Monograph Series, 1997); Howard Gardner, *Extraordinary Minds* (New York: Basic Books, 1997).

39 Jean Baudrillard, *Forget Foucault* (New York: Semiotext(e), 1987), p. 69.

40 Some leading articles on the internet and the liberal arts include Brad E. Lucas, 'Learning American Memories on the Whole World Wide Web', *The Oral History Review*, Vol. 27, No. 1 (Winter/Spring 2000), pp. 152–156; Christine Gaspar, 'Situating French Language Teaching and Learning in the Age of the Internet, *The French Review*, Vol. 72, No. 1 (October 1998), pp. 69–80; Laszlo Turi, 'Scholarly Communication Through Electronic Mailing', *The Monist*, Vol. 80 (July 1997), pp. 472–479.; Joan Grenier-Winther, 'Real Issues in the Virtual Classroom', *The French Review*, Vol. 73, no. 2 (Dec. 1999), pp. 252–264.

41 For an overview of the debates, see Robert Stevens.

42 See article.

43 George Landow, *Hypertext 2.0: The Convergence of Contemporary Critical Theory and Technology* (Baltimore and London: Johns Hopkins University Press, 1997), p. 37. See also a collection of essays based on Landow's theories in George P. Landow (ed.), *Hyper/Text/Theory* (Baltimore: Johns Hopkins University Press, 1994). Similar essays that blend theories of digital technology with French post-modernism can be found in Arthur and Marilouise Kroker, *Digital Delirium* (New York: St. Martin's Press, 1997). A rather irreverent and rhetorical take on this literary approach is Arthur Kroker and Michael A. Weinstein, *Data Trash* (New York: St. Martin's Press, 1994).

44 I am indebted for this insight to the discussion of Landow by Harold Anderson in 'Digital Ontology and the Possibility of Ethics: A Levinasian Response', unpublished doctoral dissertation, Iliff School of Theology and the University of Denver, November 1999.

45 Anderson, p. 96.

46 Stephanie B. Gibson, 'Pedagogy and Hypertext', in Lance Strate *et al.*, *Communication and Cyberspace: Social Interaction in an Electronic Environment* (Cresskill NJ: Hampton Press, 1996), p. 256.

47 Baker *et al.*, 'From Theory to Implementation'.

48 Baker *et al.*, 'From Theory to Implementation'.

49 Ray L. Steele, 'Pedagogical Issues', in Erwin Boschmann, *The Electronic Classroom: A Handbook for Education in the Electronic Environment* (Medford NJ: Learned Information, Inc., 1995), p. 28.

50 Thomas Howard, *A Rhetoric of Electronic Communities* (Greenwich CT: Ablex Publishing Corp., 1997), p. 157.

51 Similar arguments have been offered by various authors in the anthology by Warren Chernaik, Marilyn Deegan, and Andrew Gibson, (eds), *Beyond the Book: Theory, Culture, and the Politics of Cyberspace*, Office for Humanities Communication, King's College, London, No. 7, 1996.

52 Nathan Schachner, *The Medieval Universities* (New York: A.S. Barnes & Company, 1962), p. 1.

53 Schachner, p. 371.
54 Paul Lakeland, *Postmodernity: Christian Identity in a Fragmented Age* (Minneapolis: Fortress Press, 1997), p. 2.
55 Jean-François Lyotard, *The Postmodern Condition: A Report on Knowledge*, trans. Geoff Bennington and Brian Massumi (Minneapolis: University of Minnesota Press, 1988), p. 1.
56 Lyotard, p. 18.
57 Lyotard, p. 49.
58 Lyotard, p. 81.
59 Geoffrey Nunberg, 'Farewell to the Information Age', in Geoffrey Nunberg (ed.), *The Future of the Book* (Berkeley: University of California Press, 1996), pp. 127–128.
60 See Siegfried Gohr, Magritte (New York: Harry N. Abrams, 2000), book as well as Michel Foucault, *This is Not A Pipe*, trans. James Harkness (Berkeley CA: University of California Press, 1989).
61 Jay David Bolter, 'Ekphrasis, Virtual Reality, and the Future of Writing', in *The Future of the Book*, pp. 270–271.
62 Open University web page, http://www.open.ac.uk/about/.
63 See Jeremy Rifkin, *The Age of Access: The New Culture of Hypercapitalism* (New York: Tarcher/Putnam, 2000).
64 Jameson's most important works are *The Political Unconscious* (Ithaca NY: Cornell University Press, 1981) and *The Cultural Logic of Late Capitalism*.
65 Stan Davis and Jim Botkin, *The Monster Under the Bed: How Business is Mastering the Opportunity of Knowledge for Profit* (New York: Simon & Schuster, 1994), p. 67.
66 Quoted from Netscape's website at http://home.netscape,com/soloutions/education/.
67 Alice K. Johnson, 'Globalization from Below: Using the Internet to Internationalize Social Work Education', *Journal of Social Work Education*, Vol. 35, No. 3 (Fall 1999), p. 377.
68 Kurt D. Moses, David Edgerton, Willard E. Shaw, and Ralph Grubb, 'International Case Studies of Distance Learning, *The Annals of the American Academy*, p. 58.
69 *See Interactive Radio Instruction: Confronting Crisis in Basic Education*, AID Science and Technology in Development Series (Washington DC: Agency for International Development, 1990).
70 James Hall, 'Distance Education: Reaching Out to Millions', *Change* (July/August 1990), p. 40.
71 Sereen Juma, 'Bedouin Women Discover Distance Learning', *Choices*, Vol. 10, No. 2 (June 2001), pp. 14–15.
72 Jamal A. al-Sharhan, 'Education and the Satellite: Possibilities for Saudi Arabia', *International Journal of Instructional Media*, Vol. 27, No. 1 (2000), p. 56.
73 See Africa Online (May 2001), http://www.africaonline.com/site/Articles/1,10,1874.jsp.
74 Neel Ruda, 'Reaching Out to People in Eurasia', http://www.globaluniversity.edu/feature/lftl/lftl.html.

75 Phillip D. Long, 'Open CourseWare: Simple Idea, Profound Implications, *Syllabus* (January 2002), p. 12.
76 Long, p. 16.
77 Jason Ohler, 'Virtual Learning', *Technology and Learning* (November 2001), p. 18.
78 See Abraham Flexner, *Universities: American, English, German* (London: Oxford University Press, 1930), p. 305ff.
79 Margaret Wertheim, *The Pearly Gates of Cyberspace: A History of Space from Dante to the Internet* (New York: W.W. Norton, 1999), p. 228.
80 The early history of the interdependency of cyberculture and counterculture is a subject still awaiting serious historical research. Observation of their linkage was first made by renowned countercultural historian Theodore Roszak, who wrote that the original vision of the personal computer was 'to create a global culture of electronic villages cradled in a healthy natural environment – the sort of world one found scattered through the pages of the *Whole Earth Catalogue.* ' Theodore Roszak, *The Cult of Information: The Folklore of Computers and the True Art of Thinking* (London: Paladin Press, 1988), p. 247. See also Nigel Clark, 'Earthing the Ether: The Alternating Currents of Ecology and Cyberculture', in Ziauddin Sardar and Jerome R. Ravetz, *Cyberfutures: Culture and Politics on the Information Superhighway* (New York: New York University Press, 1996), pp. 90–110.
81 For a Sixtiesh and romantic sort of travelguide through the early world (i.e. early 1990s) of cybergeeks and netheads, see Douglas Rushkoff, *Cyberia: Life in the Trenches of Hyperspace* (San Francisco: HarperSanFrancisco, 1994). A typical passage: 'It's hard to know whether these people are touching the next reality or simply frying their brains. Transformation, no doubt, is occurring in either case. But no matter how much permanent damage may be taking place, there is substantial evidence that these voyagers are experiencing something at least as revelatory as in any other mystical tradition' (p. 95).
82 Rushkoff, p. 189.
83 Jean Baudrillard, *Simulacra and Simulation*, trans. Sheila Faria Glaser (Ann Arbor MI: The University of Michigan Press, 1994), p. 19.
84 Margaret Morse, *Virtualities: Television, Media Art, and Cyberculture* (Bloomington IN: Indiana University Press, 1998), p. 181.
85 See Dan Schiller, *Digital Capitalism: Networking the Global Market System* (Cambridge MA: The MIT Press, 1999). 'With the growing importance of education and training for modern industry, the fiscal crises afflicting universities, and the proliferation of information technology throughout the home, the school, the factory, and the office, the stage was set for networked educational markets to burgeon. At every level, from preschool and remedial to doctoral and crafts-based education, and in an endless variety of genres and formats, both old and new, networked educational provision furnished alluring prospective entry points for profit-making companies'. (p. 171).
86 *BLS Bulletin*, p. 4.

87 *Bachelor of Liberal Studies 1999–2000 Bulletin*, University of Oklahoma, p. 9.
88 Susan S. Nash and Robert J. Dougherty, *The Diamond Solution: Keys to Successful Online Course Development and Administration* (Norman OK: Texture Press, 1999), p. 93.
89 Email from Susan Smith Nash, July 7, 2000.
90 Email message from Susan Smith Nash, June 14, 2000.
91 Email message from Susan Smith Nash, June 21, 2000.
92 Email message from Susan Smith Nash, July 3, 2000.
93 Email message from Susan Smith Nash, July 3, 2000.
94 Jay Walker, 'The Net Net', *Context*, June/July 2000, http://www.contextmag.com/magazine/setMagazineMain.asp
95 Steffen Schmidt, Mack C. Shelley, Monty Van Wart, Jane Clayton, Erin Schreck, 'The Challenges to Distance Education in an Academic Social Science Discipline: The Case of Political Science', *Education Policy Analysis Archives*, Vol. 8, No. 27 (June 16, 2000), http://epaa.asu.edu/epaa/v8n27.
96 Stephen Talbott, 'Who's Killing Higher Education', *Educom Review*, Vol. 34, No. 2 (March/April 1999), http://www.educause.edu/ir/library/html/erm99024.html.
97 Mardell Jefferson Raney, 'Interview with Lewis Perelman', *Technos Quarterly*, Vol. 6, No. 3 (Fall 1997), http://www.technos.net/journal/volume6/3perelma.htm.
98 Michel Foucault, *This is Not a Pipe*, trans. James Harkness (Berkeley CA: University of California Press, 1982), p. 18.

Index